Seven Days in Haiti

Learning from the Meek to be a Bond-Slave of Christ

By
Michael Barrick

Introduction by
Dr. J. L. Williams, Founder and CEO
New Directions International

PRESS

Dedication

This book is offered in loving honor to the dedicated Christians of Haiti and those who collaborate with them to reclaim the land for Christ, for they are acting upon the knowledge that, "…there are still very large areas of land to be taken over" (Joshua 13:1b).

"Blessed are the meek, for they will inherit the earth"
(Matthew 5:5).

Acknowledgements

I owe deep gratitude to God for my supportive and loving family – my wife Sarah, our daughter Lindsay, and our son, Allyn. Without their full encouragement and support, I would not have had the freedom and confidence to travel to Port-au-Prince to learn from the fully surrendered Christians there what it means to be a bond-slave of Jesus Christ. A special thanks is extended to Lindsay, who designed the cover of the book.

This book would not be possible without the support of New Directions International (NDI) of Burlington, N.C. They placed faith in my ability to use the gifts, skills, talents and experiences that the Lord has given me, knowing that the trip to Port-au-Prince would lead to me being "poured out and broken." They knew that through this experience I would learn the truth of what it means to be a bond-slave of Jesus Christ.

In particular, I thank NDI Founder, Dr. J.L. Williams, as well as Joseph Williams, Robbie Hambright, Scott Hahn, Gurland Roberts, Pat Neese, and Jeff Peckham. I am sure there are many others within the organization deserving of thanks for helping to prepare my way, so though I can't mention them all, I do acknowledge their roles.

I owe a special thanks to Joseph Desrivieres, who spent virtually every waking minute providing me escort and protection as we negotiated the dangerous streets of the western hemisphere's poorest city. Thanks also to Stanley Joachim, who like John in Acts 13:5, served as an always faithful and humble aid to Joseph and myself.

A special thanks and prayer is also extended to Wes Morgan of Winston-Salem, N.C., who briefed me before my trip, and who himself has risked his life to provide aid to the Christians of Haiti. Shortly after my trip to Haiti, Wes was kidnapped in Port-au-Prince, was terrorized and suffered nearly unto death. As you read this account, you will see his name repeatedly, for he takes seriously the call to minister in the name of Jesus.

Thanks to the many Haitians who hosted me with the utmost hospitality.

It is my prayer that God blesses each of these folks – and all the people associated with NDI and the other ministries serving Haiti's Christians. I know, that when they join the Church eternal, each will hear, "Well done, good and faithful servant."

It is also my prayer that you will be moved to be part of what is occurring in Haiti because of the work and surrendered lives of Christians there. In doing so, it is you that will be blessed, just as I have been.

Table of Contents

Introduction

Haiti changes everyone. Most people travel to this poorest country in the Western Hemisphere in the hopes of helping change Haiti. But in the process, most find that they are changed far more dramatically than they change Haiti.

Over the past four decades, I have taken hundreds of people to Haiti. None have ever returned home the same. Their experiences in Haiti – whether short or long – leave an indelible impression upon their lives. This book is the graphic chronicle of one such Haiti pilgrimage.

For most travelers to Haiti, the multiple-layered culture shock goes beyond anything they could have imagined or prepared for. Within an hour of landing in Port-au-Prince, all of their senses are overloaded and maxed out from being suddenly immersed in the diverse sights, sounds and smells of Haiti. For many, the drive from the airport to their hotel or guest house is enough to push them over the sensory and emotional edge.

When you step off the plane and clear Customs in Haiti, you are soon bombarded with an intense diversity of experiences for which life in the United States leaves one unprepared. The all-encompassing press of humanity… the searing heat and soggy humidity… the strange cacophony of sounds…the maddening traffic jams of antiquated cars, tap-taps and over-laden trucks…the pot-hole filled roads strewn with garbage…the grinding poverty of the people in every direction – all slam into your five senses simultaneously and cause you to lose your emotional equilibrium. For many it is their first real experience of authentic cultural shock! They might as well have landed on Mars!

Within a few hours, many experience a level of discomfort – or panic – that causes them to want to get right back on the next departing plane and fly back to the United States as quickly as possible! Most don't. They resist the urge to "cut and run." They stick it out and are drawn deeper and deeper into the mysterious spiritual and cultural vortex known as Haiti.

Inexplicably, when many return home after their first visit, they continue to come back again and again. That's because Haiti has forever captivated their hearts. Or put more correctly, the *people* of Haiti have forever captivated their hearts. Their friendliness, smiles and warmth in the midst of such adversity is almost inexplicable.

One thing for sure, no one can say they have really experienced Haiti until they have gone to church there. The joyous singing, the fervent praying, and the passionate preaching is a worship experience that few ever experience in the United States. This 30 to 50 percent evangelical church growth is almost unparalleled in the Western Hemisphere.

But neither can you begin to understand Haiti without some knowledge of the all-pervasive presence of voodoo as the spiritual and religious bedrock of the country and culture. It is this satanic stronghold that has caused millions in Haiti through her two centuries of tumultuous history to be locked up in ignorance, superstition, poverty and fear. But the Christian Church is pushing back the kingdom of darkness through the power of the Spirit and the Word.

All of this and more is what Michael Barrick experienced in Haiti during a recent time of political turmoil. And in this book he graphically recounts his life-changing week in Haiti.

Until a couple of years ago, I did not know Michael. He worked for Wall Watchers, a Christian organization with which I was familiar. They are what we sometimes call a "watch-dog organization" that evaluates Christian ministries. This is so that the public can have an objective view of whether they are sound theologically, organizationally and financially. Previous to meeting Michael, Wall Watchers had done a "shake-down" of NDI. As a result of this investigation of us, Michael had also picked our ministry to do a further profile on in his "Shinning Light" series.

To prepare this profile, Michael made an appointment to come to our ministry headquarters for a half-day of meeting with me and our leadership staff. As we sat together, he asked us scores of questions about our mission purpose and ministry philosophy. We were as open and candid as we knew how to be. But we knew from other similar interviews the frustration and futility of trying to describe the indescribable, of trying to summarize in words what can only be experienced first hand.

Eventually I told Michael what I often tell others: "You cannot fully understand NDI from a tour of our headquarters. That's a good start, but it is not enough. You can only begin to understand us from going to one of the many countries we are involved in. It is only as you meet the key national leaders we work with and visit the projects we partner with them on, that you can begin to understand the spiritual and organizational DNA of NDI."

Without this first-hand "field experience," anyone's understanding of NDI will always be superficial. It would be like trying to evaluate a group of Special Forces by spending time with them in their barracks! While that would be helpful, it would be incomplete. To fully understand a battalion of Special Forces, you have to be "embedded" with them on the battle front to begin to get a more realistic perspective of what they do. It's the same with NDI.

Since Haiti is the poorest country in the Western Hemisphere, and one of our oldest fields of involvement, I challenged Michael to personally visit there. In time, as you will read in this book, he did. And like it has with others, it forever changed his life. But unlike most others who visit Haiti, Michael is gifted with the writing skills to recount his experiences in a captivating way.

Trained as an investigative reporter, he went to Haiti with pen and pad in hand. And while he took copious notes that became the basis of this book, God did some indelible writing on the tablets of Michael's heart at the same time! This book is the result of that dual authorship. So in the following pages, you will meet many of our dear Haitian partners. You will also learn a lot of Haitian history as well as something of the on-going contemporary political situation there. But more than anything, you will experience Haiti through the heart and daily devotional journaling that Michael did.

So it is an honor to write this forward about a country and a people that I dearly love. And even though I have visited Haiti more frequently than any other country in the world I minister in, I have freshly experienced it through the eyes, ears, heart and pen of Michael Barrick. And as you re-live a full and furious week in Haiti with him through the pages of this book, I hope you will do what he did. I hope that you too will get your passport, pack your bag and go on a life-changing "Kingdom Adventure" to Haiti with NDI or with your local church. I guarantee you will never be the same. You too will return home with the Haitian people forever etched in your mind and heart!

J. L. Williams
Founder and CEO
New Directions International
Burlington, N.C.

November, 2006

Foreword

In January, 2006, Lt. Gen. Urano Teixeira da Matta Bacellar, the Brazilian commander of the nearly 8,000 U.N. troops charged with keeping the peace in Haiti, reportedly died of a self-inflected gunshot wound. What would lead a toughened commander to take his own life?

The answer – I believe based on my visit there in August, 2005 – is hopelessness.

The evidence is overwhelming. In November, 2006, Haiti – already the western hemisphere's poorest nation – also earned the dubious distinction of being named the world's most corrupt country by Transparency International. Based on the group's Corruption Perceptions Index, Haiti's citizens are most likely of all of the world's people to be trapped in poverty and depraved conditions because of government and business corruption.

Anyone who has visited Haiti will not be surprised by this finding. What might surprise some, however, is how much hope there is despite the corruption. It is not the hope of wishing, of unfounded optimism; rather, it is the hope born in faith – faith in the One who offers not only hope, but also grace and mercy in every circumstance.

Christians in Haiti have hope. In fact, their faith is sometimes all that they have. A visit among them is quite the learning experience. One of the most powerful lessons I grasped was how arrogant I had been in anticipating the "good" I was going to do in serving as a short-term missionary journalist. It was I who was blessed –

changed even. Yet, each person I interviewed thanked me from the depths of their heart for coming to tell his or her story.

This is my heartfelt "thank you" to them in return – for teaching me, through example, how to be a bond-slave of Christ.

In Haiti, I beheld the first century Church up-close and personal. I encountered disciples fully surrendered to the call Jesus has placed upon them. There, one can see what it means to live the fulfilling of the Great Commission.

Despite the ongoing violence in Haiti, I am confident that the streets of Port-au-Prince will put out, more and more, a welcome mat to Christians. It is the result of the Holy Spirit, but also willing servants who have remained among their neighbors to share the hope found only in Jesus – regardless of the cost to them.

There is the sparse staff at Notre Maison, which cares for profoundly disabled children, scraping by with a leaky roof, a dwindling supply of formula, virtually no antibiotics and no readily available doctor.

There is Pastor Dieuseul, who ventures where even armed U.N. troops won't go.

There is J.B., an evangelist and educator that will travel anywhere and negotiate any obstacle to share the story of Jesus.

There is Pastor Jehu, who has assumed responsibility for raising two dozen boys, all rescued from abandonment and facelessness in the streets of Haiti.

There is Clerzius, who pastors an overflowing church, trying to educate neighborhood children, working as a dentist and operating a fledgling factory to provide desperately needed jobs and dignity to his workers.

There is Chavannes, a pastor and evangelical leader who was willing to accept the challenge of leading this nation with 85 percent unemployment, a devastated environment, a filthy capital, violent neighborhoods and international skepticism.

And there is Gertrude at Providence House, and Ronald of Haitian Christian Youth, and Joseph, and Stanley, and ...well, you get the point.

The work of those that were scattered from Jerusalem about 2,000 years ago continues today. It's just that in Haiti, things don't appear to have changed that much over the two millennia.

The people squeeze into the churches. On a Friday morning, people were standing outside the doors and windows of the over-crowded church to hear the Gospel; on Sunday morning, at 6:30 a.m., the back roads and alleyways were populated mainly by those carrying a Bible, dressed as to honor the Lord.

And, for the most part, they do it all with next to nothing. They must have faith, for it is just about all that they have. True, churches and ministries such as NDI are providing their Haitian partners with all they can with the limited resources available. But the poverty, the air pollution, the open trash fires on the streets, the deforested mountainsides, the under-utilized agricultural potential, the waste of human resources, the corruption, the street violence and the thousands of abandoned street children – these problems have only one solution: the Gospel of Jesus Christ.

This, however, is not news. Or at least it should not be. For Jesus told us we were going to have to go to the ends of the earth to tell His story.

Englishman William Carey, one of the first modern-era missionaries, who established the London Missionary Society in 1792, and one year later went to India, helped set the standard for missionary endeavors. Living among those he served, he partnered also with indigenous converts. Together, they translated Bibles, preached, operated schools, and provided for essential needs. As New Tribes Mission missionary Gracia Burnham noted in her book, "In the Presence of My Enemies," Carey said:

> "As a young child I learned the importance of putting my best effort into all that I did, and completing each task that I started – a discipline that was to pay off in my later years on the mission field…From the beginning God gave me the desire to know exactly what his Word said…As I continued my study and meditation on his Word, I could not help but be impressed with the fact that we, as believers, were simply not doing all that God had commanded. When his Word says,

'Go ye,' he means Go *ye*! And when he says 'into all the world,' he means into *all* the world. To 'preach the gospel to every creature' means exactly that. God means what he says. He has commanded us to 'go and make disciples of all nations.' The promise that follows is, 'lo, I am with you always.' Do any of us have the right to play leapfrog with the command and (only) hug to the promise?"

The question is not rhetorical.
No, we do not.
Of course, not every person is called to venture to foreign lands. But the harvest is plentiful and there are not many workers. But it isn't a question of lacking resources; rather, it's a matter of misdirected resources. The Church is capable of better steward-ship of mission resources. Luke wrote, "Now the Bereans were of more noble character than the Thessalonians, for they received the message with eagerness and examined the Scriptures everyday to see if what Paul said was true" (Acts 17: 11). The lesson here is that scrutiny is biblical. In my work as a journalist, I have, sadly, uncov-ered countless tales of "Christian" leaders enriching themselves with gifts intended for Kingdom purposes.

However, each of the Haitian Christians you are about to meet welcomed my presence. They answered every question. They eagerly, insistently even, opened their ministries. They were trans-parent. They – and thousands more like them in Haiti – can use your prayers. And your money if God has so equipped you. They'll put it to very good use.

Preface

"…whoever wants to become great among you must be your servant, and whoever wants to be first must be your slave – just as the Son of Man did not come to be served, but to serve, and to give his life as a ransom of many"

(Matthew 20: 26b-28).

While this book is an account of my personal spiritual growth that resulted from my encounters with Haitian Christians, it is much more. It is a challenge to believers of the Name – particularly those in the United States – to consider the faith modeled by our brothers and sisters in Haiti. No matter where you are in your Christian walk, I am confident that just as their surrendered lives helped transform my life, learning of them can do the same for you.

It is my prayer that you will consider the question from the last line of the "Utmost for His Highest" study for the last day I spent in Haiti. Oswald Chambers concluded that study with, "Are we living in such human dependence upon Jesus Christ that His life is being manifested moment by moment?"

So often today, especially in the land where our Declaration of Independence guarantees us "…the pursuit of happiness," we lose sight of the fundamental biblical principle that our lives are not our own. We forget, that as Christians, we are to live as Christ lived – "Who being in very nature God, did not consider equality with God something to be grasped, but made himself nothing, taking the very nature of a servant, being made in human likeness. And being found in appearance as a man, he humbled himself and became obedient to death – even death on a cross!" (Philippians 2: 6-8).

We must also remember what the Apostle Paul wrote about that death on the cross – "But God demonstrates his own love for us in this: While we were still sinners, Christ died for us" (Romans 5:8).

While we were still sinners! When we hated Him! While we were rebels! While we lived for own wretched purposes! It was *then* that Jesus died on the cross. Forgiveness preceded repentance!

It is easy to forget these truths in the rush of our own lives, in the land of the plenty. Here, we don't have to live moment by moment, dependent upon God – living only by faith.

In Haiti however, our brothers and sisters in Christ do.

Certainly, if they can give of themselves for His namesake, even while wondering from whence the next meal will come and living in a land that has, through the practice of voodoo, dedicated itself to the devil, we can do the same.

This is our work, our call. We are to be bond-slaves. It was Jesus, in His human likeness, who exhibited the characteristics we are to emulate. So, it is while we are here, in our mortal bodies, that we are to humble ourselves so that when our family, friends, coworkers, neighbors, and even strangers associate with us, they see lives so fully surrendered that they will be led to repentance so that they will have the assurance we have – they will not perish.

Our Lord is patient with us. The Bible tells us, "The Lord is not slow in keeping his promise, as some understand slowness. He is patient with you, not wanting anyone to perish, but everyone to come to repentance" (2 Peter 3:9).

Our lives are a journey, hopefully of spiritual growth. So, this account, while of one brief week in my life, is the telling of a journey of titanic spiritual growth that was significantly disproportionate to the short time I spent inside the country. I pray that the time you spend reading it has an impact on you as well.

Nearly two years after former President Jean-Bertrand Aristide was violently driven out of power on February 29, 2004, Haiti finally held elections. The newly-elected president is Rene Preval. The people of Haiti have spoken. The leaders they've chosen deserve an opportunity to succeed. The danger, of course, is that expectations, if not realized – especially of the impoverished that have placed their faith in Preval through the ballot box – will lead to continued instability or even worse. Conversely, a successful government brings stability and, hopefully, a safer environment for missionaries and other Christians to return to Haiti to support our brothers and sisters in Christ there.

Haitians will not escape poverty and despair with only a stable government and renewed international favor. Rather, it is only the Church that offers true hope. Jesus said, "I tell you the truth, anyone who has faith in me will do what I have been doing. He will do even greater things than these, because I am going to the Father. And I will do whatever you ask in my name, so that the Son may bring glory to the Father. You may ask for anything in my name, and I will do it" (John 14: 12-14). Yet, he added a cautionary note, "...apart from me you can do nothing" (John 15; 5c).

Progress is slow in Haiti. As Dr. Williams has noted, "Satan is not in the business of giving up real estate." He added, "Only the Church can deal with this root problem." So, it is prudent to remember, "Let us not grow weary in doing good, for at the proper time we will reap a harvest if we do not give up" (Galatians 6:9).

Astonishing Faith

*"Your love is extravagant/Your friendship, it is inti-
mate/I feel like moving to the rhythm of your Grace"
(From the Casting Crowns CD, "Casting Crowns."
Lyrics by Darrell Evans).*

The seven days in Haiti had left me exhilarated, but exhausted. I was scheduled to arrive in Charlotte, N.C. on the evening of Aug. 9, 2005.

However, before our plane even departed from Port-au-Prince that sweltering afternoon, I knew I was not going to make it to Miami in time to make my connecting flight to Charlotte, where my family was to pick me up. I was hopeful, though, that a later flight would still get me there later that evening.

The longer our plane was delayed in Port-au-Prince though, the more I came to realize that I probably would be spending the night in Miami. But there was no way to call home, as we were sitting on the tarmac.

Finally, we took off – nearly two hours late, the exact window of time I had to make the connecting flight. I was still hopeful, though, that I would make it to Miami in time to call my family and perhaps catch them before they left for the 70-mile drive to Charlotte. However, once we landed in Miami, we again sat on the tarmac in the crowded Airbus, forced to wait because our late arrival meant we simply had to be patient for the first available gate. That took nearly another hour.

So, when I did get to a phone to get through to my family, they were already in Charlotte. I was disappointed, and so were they. But our daughter Lindsay, who always has an eternal perspective, relayed a message to me through her mother. She said, "It's OK Daddy. God has a plan. There's a reason you have to spend the night there. You'll see."

My new flight was scheduled to leave at 7 a.m. After getting to the airport the next morning, I was quickly processed and sitting in a chair at the gate with nearly two hours to spare before my plane would begin loading.

I reached into my computer bag and pulled out my Bible. I turned to the book of Acts, where I had left off reading on the plane the evening before. I began reading chapter 12, the account of Peter's miraculous escape from prison. I got to verse 16, where we read of the very people who had been praying for his release. "But Peter kept on knocking, and when they opened the door and saw him, they were astonished."

I wrote this in the margin of my Bible – "Even the First Century saints, who we hold up as models of faith, did not initially see their answered prayer. It just goes to show how easy it is to doubt."

At that moment, I looked up. Standing a few feet away was a man I knew, but hadn't seen in years. A Brazilian, he had for years helped with the youth at our previous church during the time our children were in their most impressionable years. They both had grown to love him. But we had lost track of him. So, I approached him. It took him a minute to figure out who I was, but we were quickly recalling old times. I soon learned he had since moved back to Brazil. But, he was on his way to our hometown on some business.

When we got to Charlotte, Allyn and Sarah were both, well, astonished, as I had been, when I first saw Renaldo in Miami.

I learned a valuable lesson from this encounter. The First Century saints were not astonished because they lacked faith; rather, they were astonished at God's intimate involvement in our lives, including answered prayers!

That is the lesson of this book. Before I left for Port-au-Prince, I prayed with Robbie at NDI's offices. He prayed that I would be broken and spilled out. He prayed that I would learn what it means to be a bond-slave of Jesus Christ.

That prayer was answered. Appropriately, it was answered by Haitian Christians who live very much like the "followers of the Name" we read about in the book of Acts. They live day-to-day, forced to rely upon God for daily provision.

They are the "meek" we read about in the Sermon on the Mount.

They live without the creature comforts that we, who live in the United States, take for granted. The water is not safe to drink. Electricity is, at best, random. Food is scarce. Some people go days without meals. They are lacking basic medical supplies, books and other fundamental educational materials, and live in a city inundated with malaria-carrying mosquitoes. It is covered with a constant haze of smoke from mounds of trash burned on back alleyways and main drags alike.

Their city is full of cars without any exhaust emission requirements, with drivers that appear suicidal and that negotiate hilly, dust-filled streets without even the first traffic signal.

Yet, on Sunday morning, at 6:30 a.m. or before, the streets and alleyways are filled with people, dressed in the finest clothes they own, Bibles in hand, faithfully walking to their churches, often merely small block buildings with leaking roofs and half-walls.

These are their stories.

It is also a personal story, a transparent account of my own personal spiritual growth. I share much of my journaling done during the visit. The sole purpose for doing so is to point to the very personal way in which God deals with His people. Too often, we think of God as cold and distant. Admittedly, there have been times in my life when I felt that God was not even hearing me; still, I know also that God communicates intimately with us through His Spirit, His Word and His people. As this interaction was a key to the spiritual growth I experienced, it is essential to include it.

Waking early was never a problem. The crowing of the roosters ensured that. The early morning allowed time for study and reflection before we embarked upon our daily appointments. Those times of prayer played a significant role in what God taught me while there; so again, including the reflections from those pre-dawn hours is essential in communicating the spiritual growth I experienced.

Yet, it is the encounters I had with these fully surrendered Haitian Christians that had the most profound effect on my spiritual growth. They are the ones, who through their examples, taught me about true surrender to Jesus Christ. Their faith has left me astonished. It is my prayer their stories do the same for you.

August 2004 – August 2005

Preparing the Way

"Now it is required that those who have been given a trust must prove faithful"

(1 Corinthians 4:2).

Though I spent only seven days in Haiti, God was laying the groundwork for what was to happen to me there for at least a year before I went.

Sometime in the early months of 2005, I had contacted officials at New Directions International (NDI) about profiling them as a Shining Light of the Gospel for a ministry for which I worked, Wall Watchers. Through its donor empowerment website, MinistryWatch. com, Wall Watchers profiles ministries that it considers consummate examples of Christian nonprofits. These ministries must demonstrate exemplary, efficient use of the resources entrusted to them by donors, effective program management, and most importantly, a clear commitment to share the Gospel of Jesus Christ without apology.

The term Shining Light is based on the words of Jesus, "In the same way, let your light shine before men, that they may see your good deeds and praise your Father in heaven" (Matthew 5:16). Following an on-site visit to NDI, the Shining Light was published in April, 2005.

But I was not done. NDI, because of the nature of its ministry – it partners with indigenous Christians, but first puts them through a rigorous vetting process – offered to allow me an opportunity to see first-hand the work of their partners. J.L. asked me, "What would you think about going to Haiti?" He explained, "The brothers and sisters down there face incredible obstacles. If you really want to understand our ministry and how thoroughly we check and monitor our partners, and if you really want to be blessed, you must travel there."

It was more a challenge than an invitation.

Perhaps J.L. read my personality and knew I couldn't resist such a challenge. Without consulting anyone, including my family, I said, "Yes." Then I added, almost as an afterthought, "Let me pray about it."

But I didn't really need to pray about it, for God had prepared my heart the previous August, when I visited a similar ministry in Forest, Va., World Help. We had selected that ministry to be our first Shining Light. While visiting there, and seeing the faces of believers from all over the world in the pictures that line the walls and halls of the ministry's headquarters, and listening to the stories of the World Help leaders and staff about how a trip to assist foreign Christians had forever impacted their lives, I knew before I left the building that I would have to experience such a trip for myself.

It was more than a feeling; it was a calling. It was God's quiet, gentle voice using the circumstances I had just experienced and the testimonies I had just heard to speak to my heart. On that August day in 2004, I knew I would be hopping on a plane somewhere, some time to experience the exhilaration of meeting and reporting upon Christians in much humbler circumstances than I could ever experience in the United States.

I just didn't know how God would orchestrate it – until J.L. challenged me.

Day 1: Wednesday, August 3, 2005

One Purpose

First Impressions

"...you will be my witnesses in Jerusalem, and in all Judea and Samaria, and to the ends of the earth"
(Acts 1:8b).

As our plane descended over Haiti ("The land of mountains"), which accounts for about a third of the island of Hispaniola, my first impression was that I was entering a beautiful land. But as we got closer to the ground, it became apparent that the mountains surrounding this ancient port city were mostly barren. There is minimal tree canopy, and riverbeds of mud could be seen stretching down the mountain like aged fingers.

But the environmental degradation – while clearly serious – is merely symbolic of what I experienced in my seven days in Haiti – all in the nation's capital of Port-au-Prince. Consequently, this account of Haiti is not meant to be a comprehensive examination of the entire nation, or all of its woes. Rather, it is an account of how, by spending just a week there, I came to see the vital work of the Christians there, and how God, by working through them, changed my life.

The challenges facing Haiti are daunting. This is all the more reason that Christians should set our sights on Haiti – for if we involve ourselves there and commit the needs to prayer, when Haiti is rescued and reclaimed, only God can get the glory.

As I slowly descended the stairs onto the tarmac, determined to fill my senses with the moment, I was struck by the presence of U.N. troops hurrying us into the airport's terminal.

I had been warned to keep my hands on my bags. So, once I retrieved them from the carousel, and exited the front side of the terminal, I gripped them with white-knuckle fervor. I looked for the man that was to be my escort. I saw nobody that met the description I had been given of him, but then, there were dozens upon dozens of people crowding the airport entrance. Finally, a man appeared with my name on a ragged piece of cardboard. He immediately did what I had been told to not do. He handed off my bag to another person. As we scurried across the parking lot in the blasting heat, unable to communicate with one another, circumstances seemed to be quickly getting out of control.

Finally, we reached a banged-up bronze Isuzu Trooper. I attempted to grab the bag from the man who now held it as tightly as I had. He wouldn't let it go. He first wanted $10. The little money I had was designated for ministry, and I had been cautioned against allowing myself to being taken advantage of. Nevertheless, negotiation was futile and delaying seemed dangerous, so I paid.

The man who had met me at the airport entrance motioned for me to get in the front seat. Soon, others came to the window demanding money. I asked – or rather insisted – in English, that my escort get us going. I was perplexed. He didn't answer to the name Joseph, which was the name of the man scheduled to pick me up. He also didn't speak English. Another fellow with him explained, in barely discernable English phrases, that neither of them were Joseph. It was only later that I learned that the driver was recruited at the last minute because Joseph's truck wasn't running.

Though I didn't know it at first, he did not know where the guest house was. Only after we passed many of the same landmarks more than once, and as he anxiously chattered on his cell phone, did I discern that he had made numerous wrong turns en route to the guest house.

As it turned out, the meandering trip was providential, for it provided me with a tour of Port-au-Prince I would not have otherwise gotten. Up and down putrid alleyways we rode, dodging pedestrians, chickens, goats, other vehicles, and roads that haven't seen a paving truck in decades. Though we could not understand one another, it was not necessary. My initial apprehensions soon subsided. His sweet smile, his reassuring demeanor, and the simple sticker in his truck – "Jesus" – connected us like only God's Spirit can with brothers in Christ. Meanwhile, while I could not understand every word of his friend, I understood enough to know he spoke with pride of his nation.

It occurred to me that the anxiety at the airport that these two men had displayed was because of the responsibility they felt in getting me to my destination safely. I then understood that it is people like these that native and foreign evangelicals are counting on to rid this nation of the poverty, corruption and crime that can be solved only when a nation's people turn their hearts to God.

As I surveyed the streets and the people crowding them, I was overcome with a sense of shame at my initial reaction to the people at the airport. While a sense of stewardship did make me hesitant to part with the funds entrusted to me, I realized also that the men at the airport were in survival mode. They were merely attempting to earn desperately needed dollars.

My awareness and understanding grew as we traveled the squalid streets, with children wandering around aimlessly. U.N. vehicles were everywhere, along with the soldiers that staff them.

Christians there, however, are hoping for a different kind of soldier. While most are clearly thankful for the limited stability the U.N. brings, it is left to Christians to bring the Gospel of Christ here – a nation that, despite its proximity to the United States, seems to be "the end of the earth."

A Home Away From Home

"And my God will meet all your needs according to his glorious riches in Christ Jesus. To our God and Father be glory for ever and ever, Amen"
(Philippians 4:19-20).

The Scripture above greets every visitor to Providence Guest House, a guest home for Christian missionaries, pastors, evangelists and others working to fulfill the Great Commission in Haiti's unstable capital.

Operated and owned by Haitian Gertrude Bien-Aime Azor and her American partners, Rick and Sandra Sowers, Providence Guest House, established in early 2004, is an oasis of quiet, comfort and safety in this bustling, crowded, noisy, polluted and perilous city.

Because the United Nations presence is widely viewed as inefficient at best, it is arguable that what good that is being done in Port-au-Prince – and presumably all of Haiti – occurs largely by the hands of Christians.

That is why Providence Guest House is so important for the foreign guest. For the long, hard, hot and dusty days that are part and parcel of partnering with Haitian Christians, the home is a welcome sight as the sun begins to ease up from its day of baking the parched earth and people.

By even the most modest of U.S. standards, Providence Guest House does not have all of the basic needs (such as hot water), let alone the household items and appliances that U.S. citizens have come to expect as standard, but really are luxuries (such as air conditioning).

But, it is clean, the food is properly cooked and quite tasty, there is fresh bottled water and coffee in the morning. And for the journalist who is obsessive about deadlines, Providence Guest House even has Internet (when the electricity is working or the generator operating).

Still, one does have to fight off the mosquitoes with everything from bug spray to malaria pills; take a cold shower as soon as the roosters sound the alarms about 5 a.m.; place fans strategically over the bed – both for comfort and to make a breeze too strong for the mosquitoes to brave; and remember not to rinse the toothbrush with tap water.

Yet, if I'm not at home, I can think of nowhere I'd rather be.

The reason is simple. Gertrude explained, "I like to serve. This is where I find my joy." It is evident not only in the way she treats the guests – even though it is set up with dorm rooms, she will try and give everyone privacy, even if that means she and her family sleep in the upstairs hallway – but also through her cheerful and sweet employees.

The Bible verse chosen as the home's mission and greeting are not only relevant to the mission, but also symbolic of the establishment of the house, Gertrude explained, "When we started this guest house, it was an adventure to us. We even had reservations before we had the guest house. When the time came, and we were looking for a house in the area and we couldn't find anything, at the last moment we found this house. It was through that experience that we chose the verses."

She pointed out, "We are in the middle of everything and close to downtown." And, she is a very accommodating host. Because our schedule would not allow us to visit everyone we wanted to while in Port-au-Prince, Gertrude graciously opened the guest house many evenings for guests to come over for dinner before interviews. The last evening, in fact, she and her staff fed six young men while they told their stories of being rescued from the streets of Haiti by a ministry partner of NDI.

Gertrude counts it all joy. "I feel that I am in God's will."

But, she acknowledged, "It was not an easy process at the beginning." As noted, they had guests but no location, they had problems getting the beds, had to buy materials in the U.S. and the first house they had agreed upon fell through when the owner changed his mind at the last moment.

So, she prayed. "It was a Saturday. I was praying very hard and asked the Lord, 'We have everything, even the money. Is it your will to open the guest house or not?' Later, I stopped by Notre Maison (a ministry she serves as board chairperson – its story is told later) and met with the assistant supervisor to pray and meditate."

The result? They decided to go to a home just two houses away and ask the elderly man there if he would be willing to rent it. Gertrude recalled, "He said yes. We jumped on it. He had everything we needed – a generator, inverter and even beds that he wanted to sell."

She added simply, "I know the will of God is here in this."

Still, there are struggles. The vast majority of westerners are missionaries and many mission agencies have quit sending people to Haiti because of the political instability. A vacation spot it is not. Even the beautiful harbor is abandoned due to the violent neighborhood nearby, Cite Soleil. Explained Gertrude, "At the beginning, we were doing really well. Because of the political situation in Haiti, we are very slow right now."

She understands, however. "I would like to get more people to serve and help so many missionaries do their work in Haiti. However, I know to work in Haiti, you need so much patience. When you come down it is not easy."

That's why the guest house is so important to her. "When they come home from their work, they have a place they can rest peacefully. In bad times, I always smile to them to reflect the face of Christ and act just like Him. I'm not there yet, but that is my goal."

She knows also that the missionaries and the Haitians with whom they partner are doing a critical work. "The problem in Haiti is spiritual. We have to have a heart for Jesus. We need to change our hearts."

In fact, she hopes to launch a scholarship program. "I feel that Haiti needs so much. Haiti needs people that have a good education.

Illiteracy is high. In order to help, I want a scholarship program for children in the slums to go to school. Because of all what is going on in Haiti, so many injustices are done to women. Sometimes they have children with no father. In order to feed that child, they end up with more children. All of this pushed me to open a program for women. I teach them sewing and embroidery so that they can make an honorable living."

Smiling, she concluded, "My heart is for serving people. I'm glad to help, glad to make a difference in the lives of people."

Living in Darkness

*"But the way of the wicked is like deep darkness;
they do not know what makes them stumble"*
(Proverbs 4: 19).

Clerzius Liberus is the pastor of Evangelic Church of Horeb Rock (Exodus 17:6). He is also a factory owner and dentist. We had plans to visit his factory and church on Friday, but both Joseph and I agreed to use the supper hour every evening to get to know some of the folks I would be visiting. First, it would help break the ice; second it would be an efficient use of time, as I could type directly into my computer for any interviews that I conducted; but most importantly, breaking bread together affords a level of intimacy ideal for forming immediate and lasting bonds.

So, this, my first day in Haiti, we had dinner with Clerzius.

A gentle man, he described himself as a "hard preacher." But then again, some might say the same about Jesus. He was uncompromising about God's call upon his life; should a believer do any less? Clerzius, in his early fifties, does not think so.

He explained, "I was raised in a Christian family." But of course, he had his own decision to make. He recalled, "When I turned 15, I got Jesus Christ in my life." As a result, he started to preach the Gospel in a small town, and then came to the Theological Seminary of Port-au-Prince, graduating in the early 90's.

Still, being a pastor is not enough. Along with his Bachelor's in Theology, he owns the businesses and has founded a school. His small sewing factory, with about a dozen employees, serves a valuable purpose in his Kingdom-building efforts. He said, "I try to give jobs to people, because it helps with dignity. The big thing that God put in my heart is to help people."

And, he added, "Haiti is a good country, but there are so many people that don't have Jesus Christ in their life. The first thing we have to do is bring lots of people to Jesus Christ. It is the only way Haiti is going to change. There are a lot of problems with politics, but we trust in God. But if people come to Jesus Christ, I think a big, big, change comes to Haiti."

Still, the nation must overcome its cycle of poverty, insisted Clerzius. "When in poverty, people will do what they need to do to survive. It is often a bad thing. For example, there is a lot of prostitution."

Still, he does not despair. He is patient. "Well, the first step to bring someone to the Lord is to talk to them about God. First of all, that God wants to forgive their sins. After we talk, if the person has a problem, I tell them God can solve it or help them through it if they trust in Jesus."

He is apparently successful – admittedly under the complete control of the Holy Spirit. He has about 150 people attending his small church, which he hopes to expand. But, he insisted, "It's not me doing these things. My deep desire – my priority – is to preach the Gospel. That's the first job God gave me. My confidence and motivation comes from Jesus."

He added, "Sometimes God has me to preach the hard Gospel. I am not an easy man. I always see results in the church. I want the preaching to be alive before God. Sometimes when I preach I cry. Sometimes I imagine the kind of message I'm going to preach, I cry so much. I can't understand that."

Asked if it was evidence of God's Spirit living in him, he paused, leaned back in his chair, and simply nodded his head up and down as tears welled in his eyes.

So, he focuses on training disciples, making sure that new Christians are immediately put in a Bible class for new believers.

In addition to the blessings of God, he also points to his family as a source of support. He and his wife, Venamie, have two girls, Rebecca and Marsha. "My family supports me. They support me by prayer. My wife is always encouraging people to pray for the church, for me, the ministry." And he added with a hint of laughter, "She always helps keep me…focused."

Indeed, he is, as he is determined to raise a little over $37,000 U.S. dollars to double the size of his church. In the meantime, he stays busy with other ministry opportunities, busily accumulating donated supplies for his dental clinic.

But perhaps most importantly, he is devoting much of his efforts to the children of Haiti, as he has established a school here. "God put it on my heart to teach them." While he focuses on one-hour of Bible study a day with the students, he is equally concerned about their physical welfare. In short, he said, "The parents can't give them anything to eat before going to school." So, he feeds them, knowing a child with a rumbling stomach cannot focus on much of anything else. Indeed, a Haitian proverb asserts, "A hungry stomach has no ears." Then, he says, "The first thing I do is teach them the Bible."

At the time, he was serving 40 children on just $400 a month; now it is up to well over 100. Why? He said, "The parents are very happy. They see a change in their children. We're not only feeding food, but also the Bible. Many things change as a result." He also needs money to pay the teachers, so that the children will have the highest quality education possible. That would take about $100 per month, per teacher. Presently, he operates the school with six teachers, two cooks and a secretary, all generally volunteering their time.

Yet, he noted, "But feeding is first thing, because sometimes they don't have anything for a day, but if they come to school they will know they have something to eat."

Still, he says, Bible study is crucial. "That's my priority, to lead children to Christ. I never talk to the children without talking to them about coming to Christ."

While he needs help to continue his school and add on to his church, and would welcome it, he also wants potential donors to do so prayerfully. "It would be a pleasure for me for American

Christians to know what we're doing. They can choose for themselves whether to help me."

While he is proud of his factory, he utilizes it, too, as a witnessing tool. "The first thing I tell them is that I am a pastor. Once I have done that, I can introduce them to God. When I tell them I'm a pastor, they realize the standards of industry come from God."

This is a message that they – and all Haitians – must hear, argued Clerzius, "The last president (Jean-Bertrand Aristide) gave the country to Satan." Indeed, it is widely reported that Aristide regularly allowed voodoo "worship" in the presidential palace. As a result, said Clerzius, "Every area in Haiti has a bad spirit." He was hopeful that evangelical pastor Chavannes Jeune, who ran for president, would be elected. "He will claim Haiti for Christ. I know it. He will do that."

Noting then that Chavannes faced an uphill battle, Clerzius said that regardless of the political situation, "I keep my hope by faith. I know who is God. God stirs me in His Word. What He says is true."

The Big Compelling of God

"Now to him who is able to do immeasurably more than all we ask or imagine, according to his power that is at work within us"
(Ephesians 3:20).

The first leg of the trip to Haiti began with a flight to Miami very early on this first of seven days. So, Sarah and I – rather than having to leave our home in the middle of the night to get to the Charlotte airport – spent the night in a hotel nearby the airport. I caught the first shuttle from the hotel and, looking through the window of the van, waved goodbye to Sarah, standing at the window of our room, which overlooked the parking lot.

It was the most emotional parting of our 25-plus years of marriage.

That early departure, combined with the hectic pace of the day from the moment I set foot in the van until I reached Providence House in Port-au-Prince, had kept me from finding time to read and write in my journal. Finally, after unpacking at the guest house, and while waiting on Joseph to arrive, I opened it.

The study for August 3 was titled, "The Big Compelling of God." I perked up. Next, I read the Bible verse for the study: "Behold, we go up to Jerusalem" (Luke 18:31). At this point, I got what I term "Holy Ghost bumps." I was eagerly – urgently even – now anticipating what message God had for me from this day's study. The study opened, "Jerusalem stands in the life of our Lord as the place where he reached the climax of His Father's will. 'I seek not Mine own will, but the will of the Father which had sent me.'"

I underlined the phrase and circled the word, "sent." Despite all the apprehension leading to the trip, despite the obstacles, despite the hassles such as taking malaria pills, and despite the emotion of the morning's parting with Sarah, God, in His grace, had confirmed for me that He had sent me to Haiti. Even his timing was perfect, as the verb tense of word would not have been as meaningful to me had I read the study when first awakening, as I normally do.

I read on, "He steadfastly set His face to go to Jerusalem." At that point, though I had not yet met Joseph, I lifted a silent prayer that God would guide every step of my guide – and soon to be companion – and that we would have steadfast unity of purpose.

It continued, "The great thing to remember is that we go up to Jerusalem to fulfill God's purpose, not our own." It was at this point – before I had written the first word or had met the first person that I was scheduled to meet – that I began to be poured out and broken. I was overwhelmed at how God's Spirit was going before me even in my thoughts and study.

Further into the study, I read and underlined, "We have no conception of what God is aiming at, and as we go on it gets more and more vague." A verse entered my mind: "Now to him who is able to do immeasurably more than all we ask or imagine, according to his power that is at work within us" (Ephesians 3:20). Again, an unuttered prayer was lifted. I simply praised God, for I didn't know what else to do. I did know, however, that I was at the beginning of a journey for which I could not even conceive the meaning and significance.

Next, I read, "At the beginning of the Christian life we have our own idea as to what God's purpose is – 'I am meant to go here or there,' 'God had called me to do this special work;' and we go and do the same thing, and still the big compelling of God remains." I sat at the table on the porch overlooking the alleyway. I stared across the rooftops to the mountains in the distance, humbled that I would presume to know what God had planned for me. I knew that I was simply to be available and sensitive to His Spirit.

Day 2: Thursday, August 4

Not for Our Own Cause

With Wide Open Arms

*"Come to me, all you who are weary and burdened,
and I will give you rest"*

(Matthew 11:28).

In Haiti, where the Church seems more first century that 21st century, believers serve the most unfortunate of this city's downtrodden – profoundly disabled children.

Nadia Belizaire, the nurse at Notre Maison (Our House), which cares for and ministers to approximately 30 children from ages five to 22, said, "If you weren't born handicapped, it is by the grace of God. If you are able to work, be healthy and be active, it is by the grace of God. If you are so blessed and can help these children, God will bless you."

Indeed, a visit here is a blessing. While one would not likely trade places with any of the children, there is no question that they are blessed, and bless others. Even language barriers were irrelevant, as when the visit to this home was concluding, the soft, angelic voices of some children singing "The Old Rugged Cross" in Creole drifted down the stairs, as if carried on the gentle breeze directly down from heaven. The tune – and its message – spoke volumes as to the hope that is within these children, an incredible testimony considering their circumstances.

But that is not surprising, for the house is aptly named. It truly is a home for these children.

Director Arlain Ducatel explained, "The goal of Our House is to give these children that sense that they are at home. Even though they are handicapped, it is a family setting."

The home, begun in 1993 by American missionary Ruth Zimmerman, and now run by Arlain and Manager Jeanise Celin – both Haitian, as is all the staff – is hidden away in a lightly traveled street in the center of Port-au-Prince.

Though Arlain had been director for only three months at the time of my visit, one would suspect he's spent his life here, with the zeal for excellence of which he speaks. Most notable though, is his passion. "It feels good working here. The thing that motivates me is that I am not better than the handicapped. I could be likewise. God has given me an opportunity to serve these children, to make them feel loved, to be part of a family."

Added Jeanise, "Our goal is to really give these children a place where they feel like they are living."

For a visitor, there is no mistaking that. From classrooms to music to physical therapy, all is done with large smiles and even a sense of merriment, as evidenced by the singing and dancing one staffer was doing for the enjoyment of the children. Meanwhile in the classroom, children were eagerly helping one another in groups at tables.

Nadia acknowledged that though there is joy, the work can be overwhelming. "When I first started, it really troubled me to see the condition they are in. But, as I've gotten to know them, I simply treat them as my own children." She added, "The reward is how much love the children want to give. Even the ones that are not able to speak express their love. They open their arms wide for hugs."

She spoke also of how the children respond to prayer. "One thing we do every morning is pray with them. Before breakfast, we pray. They will not touch their food until praying because they are so excited about the prayer."

While the ministry is in need of so many supplies – as is seemingly the case with every mission endeavor here – Arlain still has big dreams. "The dream is to make Notre Maison well-known nationally and internationally, to be able to make this place really a home for the children and staff."

Board chairwoman Gertrude Bien Aime Azor, who also co-owns Providence House just down the street, said she would like to get another home to separate the children as they get older. But until then, she is motivated by what seems to drive the whole staff. She explains simply, "My heart is to help the little ones."

But there are more immediate – even critical – needs. Because electric service is so sporadic and unpredictable here, the need for a bigger generator and an inverter is essential. Gasoline is expensive, and refrigerated items can easily spoil – wasting their very limited resources – if the generator is not operating properly or lacks enough capacity. The home's budget is also impacted by this unpredictable nature of electric service, as gasoline for the generator – while essential – is more expensive than electricity.

That is but the beginning. On their shelf was just one bottle of formula left for the entire house. Medicine, particularly antibiotics, was virtually exhausted. Cell phones would be helpful so that staff members can communicate when taking a child to the hospital, and gloves, gowns, and hygiene products are also needed.

And, they'd like a doctor too that could come around at least once or twice a week. That is because the hospitals here are so crowded that a wait of hours is likely, which is very difficult on children that need to adhere to a strict diet or simply not be exposed to the many diseases of the other hospital patients. Finally, driving through Port-au-Prince, which has no traffic signals, ranges from harrowing to downright deadly. Transporting disabled children to the hospital is clearly an additional risk and burden.

Yet, Arlain remains hopeful. "Yes, there are a lot of challenges, but with unity, collectivity, we will be able to overcome the challenges, especially with God as our guide. He will make it possible. We have the capable and willing staff."

While many missionaries and others visit here, raising support is very difficult, prompting Arlain to acknowledge, "Working with challenged children is not easy and there are a lot of obstacles to face. But, the willingness is there. We are available, but without proper support, we are limited in our ability to make the children and staff feel at home."

Gertrude also dreams of one day opening a large compound, where there could be homes for each age group. She is confident the right people are in place. "They have a sense of ownership. I would say that is because they are Christians. The first question we asked in the interview was, 'Are you a Christian?'"

If the joyful singing of the children is any indication, Arlain and his staff are not merely Christians. They are fully surrendered to the Lord who saved them so that they can serve these children.

Haiti's Real Struggle

"For our struggle is not against flesh and blood, but against the rulers, against the authorities, against the powers of this dark world and against the spiritual forces of evil in the heavenly realms"
(Ephesians 6:12).

After visiting Notre Maison, Joseph said that we were going to go on a sight-seeing tour, for visiting Cite Soleil was out of the question because it was too dangerous. The pastor serving in the slum would visit us for dinner at the guest house this evening instead, so Joseph suggested the tour as an alternative.

I was disappointed, for I did want to see Cite Soleil myself. Indeed, I felt that not going was a failure as a journalist. But Joseph was insistent. I certainly had to trust his judgment, and I also recalled my prayers from the previous afternoon. I knew God had put me under Joseph's protection and authority, and I knew that Joseph was not only practical, but sensitive to God's leading.

So, a sight-seeing trip it was.

At first, there were streets full of burning trash, drivers that can kindly be called rude, neighborhoods with homes where every house was surrounded by walls that have piles of rocks and pulverized gravel shoved up against them. Joseph explained that people could avoid paying taxes on property so long as the walls and homes weren't painted, and so long as they appeared to be under construction.

Soon, those piles of gravel were to become far more significant.

I vividly recall a child, maybe two- or three-years-old, drinking water that was coming up out of a pipe in a sidewalk. Not an adult or older sibling appeared to be nearby. I asked Joseph about this. He said, matter-of-factly, "He's probably a street child, abandoned by parents that can't afford to feed him or just don't want to care for him."

I was overwhelmed with my feelings of impotence in the face of such poverty and abandonment.

We continued on our tour. Joseph explained that we were going to go to the high mountaintop that could be seen from the back porch of the guest house. "From there," he offered, "you will be able to see all of Port-au-Prince. It will be quite eye-opening."

However, several minutes after we had begun our steep ascent up the winding, narrow and rough streets, a pick-up in front of us hauling cooking oil hit a bump and a huge drum of oil overturned, pouring into the street – dead in the center of a steep, hairpin turn.

I sat in the front of the truck, dumbfounded at the carnage occurring before my eyes. One vehicle after another coming down the hill hit the oil and slammed into a wall, or a pole, or another vehicle – this, despite the fact that one of the men from the truck that had overturned the oil was standing in the curve, pleading with drivers to stop.

Meanwhile, drivers behind us grew impatient as well, and passed us. They too wrecked. Soon, directly in front of us, was a pile-up that made a demolition derby seem like a casual drive on a back country road. Our truck was too large to turn around. It was irrelevant anyway. There were simply too many wrecked vehicles.

Yelling at one another in French or Creole, the drivers would get out, look at the damage, and then drive on down the mountain. Others would spin their tires, bumping walls on each side, determined to continue on up the mountain.

I was told to stay put. Joseph stayed behind the wheel, but Stanley walked up to the curve. Concerned that Stanley could be injured by the reckless drivers, I asked Joseph if perhaps we shouldn't try and figure a way to back down. That would be impossible he replied. I knew he was right. Silently, I was praying. In fact, I was biting my tongue. "OK God," I thought. "I trusted Joseph. You knew this was going to happen. What is so important about getting to the top of this mountain?" I wasn't asking just out of curiosity. I was, I admit, literally doubting God's judgment. I wasn't too sure about Joseph either at this point. I continued to pray. God, though He didn't have to answer me, did so with that still, silent voice – "Trust Me."

I mentally stepped back and acknowledged that Joseph could not have anticipated this. He was proud of his nation. He wanted me to see its beauty. In fact, he had promised, in explaining why he wanted to take this diversion, "Port-au-Prince is not just slums. It is beautiful as well. It is not just what you read about in the American press. I want you to see that." So, though I had no choice anyway, I took a deep breath – literally and spiritually – and managed a smile in anticipation of what God was going to do, though at this point I had no idea what that might be.

This is when the pulverized rock became vital. Stanley, in his ingenuity, had talked the drivers of the other truck into using an empty bucket they had to throw the rock onto the oil. Almost as fine as sand, it neutralized the oil slick. It would have worked easier had the drivers not been so impatient and rude, but as I was soon to figure out, God wanted me to witness their behavior as well, for it was to become quite revealing to me in a short period of time – though at the moment, I was angry with them, for they were endangering not only themselves, but the other drivers, Stanley, and the other men trying to fix the problem.

Finally, the mayhem was cleared and Joseph, demonstrating incredible driving capabilities, maneuvered the truck – with Stanley standing in the curve guiding him – over and around the oil spill. We had to drive several hundred yards to a relatively level area and wait for Stanley to get back to us, breathless and dusty.

We continued on up the mountain. I glanced out of the left corners of my eyes over to Joseph, wondering what sort of man he was. Resolute was the word that immediately came to mind.

He was determined I would see Port-au-Prince from this mountaintop. The reason was not clear to me, but it didn't matter.

A bond of trust began to develop. An old ambulance driver and a NASCAR fan, I was awed by his driving skills. More importantly, Joseph was on a mission appointed on to him by God – getting me to the top of the mountain, for reasons he didn't even fully understand – and nothing was going to stop him.

About 20 minutes later, after one hairpin turn after another, and with breathtaking views – steep, narrow views just below my window – we came to the top. We parked. We walked out onto a vista.

We leaned on the railing and Joseph began to point out landmarks. I peppered him with questions. I wanted to get my bearings as well. I don't know why, but whenever I visit a new place, I want to learn as much as I can about its geography and geology. Also, having grown up in the mountains, I have always looked to find the highest point. It's as if I'm planning an assault and I want the best vista possible.

It was at this point that it occurred to me that this habit of mine was metaphorical. I shared with Joseph a flood of thoughts that entered my mind after we stood there for more than an hour and talked. One notion that I entertained was that I was to launch an assault of sorts – I was to write about what God had revealed to me from not only the mountaintop, but from the experience on the way up. I shared with Joseph what I was thinking. He just looked at me. I concluded that he was beginning to have the same sort of doubts about me that I had allowed to creep into my mind about him as we had sat motionless for 45 minutes in the curve below. Instead, he broke the silence. He asked softly, of all that I had shared with him as a result of this mountain visit, "Will you remember this? Will you be able to write it all down when we get back?"

I assured him I would. He said, "Good. You must. Do it tonight before you go to sleep. It is important."

I did. The following is what I learned from my mountaintop experience.

While standing atop a high summit overlooking Port-au-Prince, it became clear to me that the problem in Haiti is spiritual. There is an extensive U.N. presence that is seemingly ineffective and costly, yet with no exit strategy. They are there because of political unrest and hundreds of kidnappings by the gangs controlling the city's slums; but as J.L. has pointed out, the U.N. is dealing with "The fruits of the problem, not the roots."

Four out of five Haitians are unemployed. The beauty of the port, the fertile valley to the east of here, and the mountain ranges on both sides truly provide this city with all the natural protection and beauty to make it appealing to those involved in commerce and tourism. Most importantly, the streets are brimming with industrious street vendors, small business owners and others trying to merely subsist. In short, Port-au-Prince has the natural resources – both physical and human – to be a thriving metropolis.

However, as I looked out over the entire city from thousands of feet above, there were two telling pictures. First, the port itself was virtually empty of ships. Except for a lone oil tanker and a few fishing boats, the huge harbor was empty. There was absolutely no activity on the water. Meanwhile, the airport appeared to be two abandoned strips of concrete. For more than an hour, not one plane – commercial or private – landed or took off from the airport.

Is there any other nation so close to the United States where the capital – from a distance – looks like a ghost town? It is inconceivable that the capital city of a nation – especially one with a protected harbor – would have virtually no ships or aircraft arriving.

But there is a reason. Two hundred years ago, the nation adopted voodoo as a religion. And, former president Jean Bertrand Aristide reportedly allowed such worship in the nation's presidential palace. In short, it is a nation whose leaders in 1804 officially committed the country to Satan in exchange for his perceived help in liberating them from French control. Indeed, Haiti was once considered "the jewel of the Caribbean," with beautiful beaches and mountains. It was rich in commerce, but that came at a price, as the French colonial rulers treated the slaves "imported" from Africa with particular harshness and cruelty. So, one can understand why the newly liberated Haitians rejected all things embraced by the French – including their Christian faith.

It is not surprising then that so many here live in horrific circumstances. Block shacks, seemingly piled one on top of the other, dot the hillsides everywhere. From the mountaintop view, one can see how tightly packed the people are between the two mountain ranges.

Paved streets are a rarity. The infrastructure is crumbling – literally. Homes, streets and even hillsides defiled by deforestation look like ancient ruins. If a nation's largest capital city is in a virtual state of anarchy, not much hope can be offered for those living there, let alone in the distant mountains.

Unless, of course, they hear about – and accept – Jesus Christ.

Fortunately for the people of Haiti, there is a concerted, focused effort by Christians both native and foreign determined to claim this land for Christ. It began in the bicentennial year of Haiti's independence with a crusade, "Haiti at the Cross." Evangelists spread out throughout the nation, and even planted a cross on the lawn of the presidential palace.

Daily, in gang-controlled areas like the neighborhood Cite Soleil, Christians risk it all to bring the Gospel where voodoo priests and priestesses are revered. Ironically, the slum's name, which is French, means Sun City in English. Located by the sea, the neighborhood – actually it is more of a city on to itself with about 300,000 residents jammed into a tiny area – would be a developer's dream in any other nation.

Protestant Haitian pastors have formed alliances, even fielding candidates for president.

But everyone with whom I spoke acknowledged the solution is not political. While they believe it would surely be better to have an authentically-committed Christian as president, they know that the problems here run as deep as the heart of each individual.

Yet, all the pastors spoke of the hope they have for their nation and its people. The hope is real, because it has been four generations (biblically speaking) since the founding of Haiti in 1804. The curse can be overcome now.

So, there is a sense of urgency here. Even a pastor in Cite Soleil (you will read about him next), despite daily threats to his life, says he feels most alive when he is ministering to the people in his community.

Indeed, they are an inspiring example. Just as Jesus came into a world hostile to his message, His disciples here today are doing the same thing.

They understand, as Paul wrote, "For our struggle is not against flesh and blood, but against the rulers, against the authorities, against the powers of this dark world and against the spiritual forces of evil in the heavenly realms" (Ephesians 6:12).

So, while the nation is in desperate need of reform and basic human necessities, Haiti's Christian leaders do not lack faith, hope and courage. So, as you consider the plight of this nation, respond as Paul counseled. "… pray in the Spirit on all occasions, with all kinds of prayers and requests. With this in mind, be alert and always keep on praying for all the saints" (Ephesians 6:18).

Facing the Enemy Head-On

"Submit yourselves, then to God. Resist the devil, and he will flee from you"

(James 3:7).

The Rev. Dieuseul Estivene ventures where even armed U.N. troops won't go. But then, Dieuseul, 50, points out that he has protection – the full armor of God.

Still, he is prudent. He insisted that our conversation be conducted at Providence House, for he – and many others – said it was too dangerous in Cite Soleil for a visit. It was pointed out that, though a journalist might be able to get in and out safely, anyone seen with him could later become a hostage. The "bad guys," say residents, will see a foreigner and presume they have plenty of money, so will perhaps later kidnap whoever accompanies him and demand that "their friend" pay ransom. Also, some westerners, such as Wes Morgan (see the Acknowledgements section) have indeed been kidnapped.

Pastor Dieuseul (translation: "God only"), conveys a gripping story.

His ministry – a school and feeding program – is serving about 450 children. For them, it is generally the only meal they get during the day. And it is unquestionably their only hope for a decent education – and hence a possible avenue of escape from Cite Soleil.

Dieuseul noted, "The thing is that during the summer vacation, we have to keep those children busy or else the bad guys will use them on the street."

Yet, Dieuseul has reported that the funding for the program, which was being provided by a U.S. businessman through two ministries, has been discontinued. That is nearly $4,300 a month he no longer receives for the feeding and teaching programs, even though the needs only grow.

He offered, "That is why we are constantly praying."

Yet, he is not critical of the decision to stop the funding. In fact, he seems to be energized by the challenge – the need to rely only upon God. "I feel alive when I am over there. I am hoping and waiting for a change to take place in that area by the grace of God. As I pray, I already foresee God taking care of that situation. While it is true the support has ended, I still have hope."

The school was started in 1981 with 10 children – and when the neighborhood was safe and friendly. It now has nearly 400 students from age three to 14, though they are feeding even more. They do so with just him, his wife Magda who is a registered nurse, and five employees, including his brother Dieujuste (translation: "God is Just"), who is the school's director.

Indeed, Cite Soleil is notoriously dangerous, with gangs controlling much of it despite the presence of U.N. troops. "That's the problem we're facing with U.N. They are not able to take control," said Dieuseul. "We're not at war with another country. This is a situation among ourselves and if they would come in and start shedding blood, I am sure the international court would judge them." He added that the U.N. needs to identify how it can best help. "If the U.N. guys would come in and work on infrastructure, it would begin to address some of the problems."

In the midst of it all, he faces the enemy head-on. It is his passion for the children and their families that spurs him on. "The school building can only take so many kids. A family may have five children, and we can only take two. The other three have no hope for food. Sometimes, the children in the feeding program will hide food in their pockets to take to their siblings."

The school does more than feed children though. "It stimulates them to be industrious," said Dieuseul. "That's why the school is so important, so that they can sustain themselves. We are trusting the Lord, as a lot of people are being blessed and being saved."

"In the old days, around the (Francois) Duvalier regime (he served as president from 1957-1971), it was a calm area," explained Dieuseul. "It was someplace people wanted to be. People respected one another. It was a strategic area when you came form the north of Haiti. It used to be a place you would stop. The area was a transit area for people migrating from the north, until they could get on their feet and move somewhere in Port-au-Prince. That's why the area is one of the biggest ghettos. It has absorbed a lot of people that come for a better life in Port-au-Prince."

He continued, "It started to really degrade after 1986. It became a political issue. From then on, many different governments who got elected never did everything." It was in 1986 that Jean-Claude Duvalier was forced from power. Military leaders, many of whom were corrupt themselves, nevertheless objected to the brutality of Duvalier and reportedly forced him to leave at gunpoint in February of that year.

A series of politicians succeeded Duvalier. Then in 1991, Jean-Bertrand Aristide became president, serving until 1994. He also served in 1996 and from 2001, until he was forced into exile on February 29, 2004 as rebels planned an attack.

Aristide, a former Catholic priest, was popular among some segments of society, but was also accused of abuses. "He used to have a feeding program for the street children. He had a theology of liberation and used to talk a lot about sharing," recalled Dieuseul. "A lot of people came to believe in him. He knows how to talk, to attract people to listen to him. That's why a lot of people, regardless of their background, believe in him."

Despite the danger, Dieuseul, who graduated from the Port-au-Prince Theological Seminary in 1987, remains hopeful. "As a citizen, pastor and a lawyer, we know that God can change the situation. The problems that are social and economic we know can be resolved in that sense."

He added, however, "If you have a crowd that has no food to eat, no water to drink, no job, no place to live, those that can do prostitution will be prostitutes. Those that can steal will start robbing people. Those people that don't have a good education and can't read are discriminated against and insulted, fueling their anger, for they can't feed their family."

He continued, "Especially right now, if we did a survey, we would have less and less pastors willing to go into that area. That has led me to really ask, what is a calling? If God called you to be at a certain place, no matter what the obstacle is, then you must answer. I don't regret that God put me in Cite Soleil. I asked God to give me strength to be an example for the children, because they need role models especially in the situation they are in with the unrest."

That does not mean there are not harrowing days. "Sometimes on our way to open the school, we will hear gunshots. Sometimes we park elsewhere so we don't get hit by a bullet. We have seen God's protection through all these things; we feel we are called by God to be here. Some of the people come to us, and say, 'If it wasn't for you, I probably would have been dead by now.' But all the glory goes to Jesus."

Despite the many hardships, and the challenge of operating without funds, Dieuseul is anticipating that the ministry will grow. "The mission in Cite Soleil has broadened our vision to extend to other areas." So, from a single church – the Evangelical Berean Baptist church in Cite Soleil – they have begun a satellite church that has about 500 members.

The story of that church helps one to understand why Dieuseul keeps a strong faith in the face of apparent hopelessness. That's because the land for the second church was purchased for $30,000, even though they had virtually no money when they determined to purchase the land.

He explained, "We are people of faith. When we claimed the land for the second church, we had about $12. We bargained with them to pay for that land in four terms. We didn't have the money, but did it by faith."

Friends paid the first portion, and two U.S. citizens paid the second and third portions. At that point, however, they still only had about half of it paid for. They had no idea where the money would come from. But early in 2005, while in Boston to speak at Harvard University about poverty, he preached at six churches. He preached at one in the morning. When the evening speaker had to cancel, the church asked him if he could preach again. He shared, "That's how one of the missionaries in the church came in and invited me to the pastor's office. I had never met the person before, and he asked me, 'How much money do you owe?' My heart pounded. It was $14,000. And he said, 'God told me to help you.' He wrote a check for $14,000."

Now they are building on the land, but need $19,000 to complete the project.

And, there is more. He has been offered the opportunity to buy more land. He explained, "There is a piece of land, promised land, in a different city, Croix des Bouquets (translation: 'Cross of Flowers')." It is there, on the approximately 20-acre lot, that Dieuseul envisions a self-sustaining community of farmers with housing, churches, schools and professionals. He added, "The same God that helped us with this land, I am sure He is able to give us the promised land."

Still, he appealed to Christians to prayerfully consider if God would use them to help his dreams become a reality. Recalling a visit by U.S. resident traveling with NDI on a "Kingdom Adventure" – in which they work with indigenous partners – Dieuseul said, "One of the testimonies is that they had fed a child. After she ate, and they saw sadness in her face, one of them asked, 'What is wrong with you?' She said, 'I was just thinking I would be dead now if not for the feeding program.'" He continued, "It is biblical what we are doing. We are helping the needy. As Jesus said, 'If you give a little one a glass of water, it is I you give a glass of water to.'"

He concluded, "I believe in God and I believe in education. The people, if they don't have God and education, it will be hard for them to get out of the situation they're in. The love that God put in my heart for them, I would like for them to live the same way I am living."

Truly a 'Kingdom Adventure'

"I feel the pain but it still doesn't change who you are/Nothing I feel is outside the reach of your arms."(Lyrics by Jill Phillips and Andy Gullahorn from "Grand Design," from Phillips' CD, "Writing on the Wall").

I had much to write after my first full day in Haiti.

That morning, however, before walking up the street to visit Notre Maison, I had begun what would be a morning ritual – awake with the roosters about 5 a.m., get a cold shower, go down and grab a cup of coffee brewed by the thoughtful and early-arriving staff, step outside on the back porch to gaze upon the mountains to pray, and then go up to top of the stairs out front, sitting on a pillow to read my Bible and do my study in "My Utmost for His Highest."

NDI calls the trips it arranges for donors and those interested in mission work, "Kingdom Adventures." The first thing I wrote in my journal that morning – before even reading it, and before even going on the adventures described above, was, "This is truly a kingdom adventure." Those words were penned based only upon my experiences from the day before and as a result of the moving of God's Spirit I felt as I enjoyed that first cup of coffee in Haiti as I watched the sun rise from the back porch and the shadows move across the distant mountain.

The study began, "The bravery of God in trusting us! You say – 'But He has been unwise to choose me, because there is nothing in me; I am not of any value.' That is why He chose you. As long as you think there is something in you, He cannot choose you because you have ends of your own to serve; but if you have let Him bring you to the end of your self-sufficiency then He can choose you to go with Him to Jerusalem, and that will mean the fulfillment of purposes which He does not discuss with you."

I underlined this passage, and double-underlined the last seven words.

I continued reading. Chambers continued, "The comradeship of God is made up out of men who know their poverty. He can do nothing with the man who thinks that he is of use to God. As Christians we are not out for our own cause at all, we are out for the cause of God, which can never be our cause. We do not know what God is after, but we have to maintain our relationship with Him whatever happens."

The passage also includes, "The main thing about Christianity is not the work we do, but the relationship we maintain and the atmosphere produced by that relationship."

Again, I underlined this section, totally ignorant at that point of the atmosphere I was to experience that day.

After reading the selection, there were not enough lines to capture all of my thoughts, so after filling up the allotted space, I wrote in the margins.

Having just finished my first cup of coffee – a ritual I am accustomed to doing with Sarah – I wrote, "I had no idea how much my morning conversations with Sarah meant until this morning and I can't see or call her." I added, "I was overwhelmed this morning as I stood on the back porch at Providence House and realized I could talk to God, regardless of where I am. He has showered me with riches, yet I am so undeserving."

In direct response to the study I wrote, "As I look at the poverty around me, it serves as a good illustration of what it means to 'know their poverty.' Until I saw Haiti, I had not seen poverty at this level; now, I am aware of it. In similar fashion, God has allowed me to see the 'poverty' of my soul. It is only then that I realize how much I need Him. It is then He uses me, just as He is now here in Haiti."

I had time also to read from the The Leadership Bible given to me by my daughter on Christmas, 1998. Based on the passage from Chambers, I turned to the section, "Dependence on God." After reading some of the notes from the section, I dated it 8/4/05 – Port-au-Prince, and wrote, "I am overwhelmed with God's grace this morning as I realize that God – by His grace – has waited for me to depend upon Him."

Also in the Bible that evening, I read Acts 8: 9-13, about Simon the Sorcerer. As I did, I recalled the story that Dieuseul told after dinner about the voodoo doctor that "competed" with him in Cite Soleil. I wrote, in the margin beside the text, "I pray the same thing occurs with Dieuseul with the voodoo priest in Cite Soleil."

At some other point during my visit, I read from Acts 16: 19. Here, Paul and Silas caused a fortune-teller to lose money by exorcising a demon. I thought again of Dieuseul, who because his faith is authentic, threatens the voodoo priests and priestesses because they make income for their incantations and "powers." So, I prayed for his protection.

Again, at some other point, probably in the Miami airport, I was reading from Acts 26. "I am sending you to them to open their eyes and turn them from darkness to light, and from the power of Satan to God, so that they may receive forgiveness of sins and a place among those who are sanctified by faith in me" (Acts 26: 17b-18). Again, I simply wrote Dieuseul's name over the text and drew an arrow to it.

In short, even though some of the reflections from my Bible study did not occur the same day as these visits, as I read Scripture, God's Spirit would instantly connect the dots for me and convict of the need to pray for these saints, which had taught me they were sacrificing it all – but not for their own cause.

Day 3: Friday, August 5

Eager to Share and Hear the Gospel

Haiti's Billy Graham

"He has showed you, O man, what is good. And what does the Lord require of you? To act justly and to love mercy and to walk humbly with your God"
(Micah 6:8).

I met Chavannes Jeune, an influential Haitian Christian leader, pastor and evangelist, just weeks before he formally announced his candidacy for president of Haiti.

In the interview at his office in the nation's capital, Chavannes said his motivation was simple. "I have the vision that our Christian people can make a positive change."

While such a view is supported by the many Haitians I was graced to meet, the violence in wake of the elections on February 7, 2006 – and the worldwide press coverage of the resulting anarchy throughout Haiti, in particular Port-au-Prince – could certainly cause some to characterize Chavannes's outlook as optimistic.

Chavannes, despite being well-known and having a solid base of evangelicals to draw upon, was unable to garner enough support to achieve victory. Still, he ran a respectable campaign, and was among the top vote getters, finishing in the top half-dozen or so, quite a feat considering that dozens were on the ballot.

While his motivation to seek the presidency might have been uncomplicated, fixing this nation's problems will be an entirely different story for President Rene Preval, since Haiti is the most impoverished nation in the western hemisphere, and where even safe, clean water is a rarity and 20 percent of children die before the age of five. Garbage pickup is virtually nonexistent, causing an odor and haze to hang over Port-au-Prince because people are constantly burning trash. And, what isn't burned litters virtually every street, alleyway and streambed.

Still, with an estimated 40 percent of Haitians being evangelicals, Chavannes believed his candidacy offered promise. However, he was unable to convince Christians to register and vote in unity, a task complicated in a nation jaded by two centuries of often corrupt leadership.

In reality, despite being only the second nation in the western hemisphere to gain its freedom, and the first to do so with a successful slave revolt, Haiti is not really independent, insists Chavannes. "After so many years of independence, our nation is still in bondage," he said.

The reason it is not truly free, he said, is because the nation was dedicated by a voodoo priest at its liberation. However, Chavannes, who is the pastor of Mission Evangelical Baptist Church, and has been involved in leadership of a number of Haitian evangelical and pastoral organizations, including as a leader in the Baptist Evangelical Mission of South Haiti, is also hopeful because of the people he serves – though he will continue to do so spiritually, whether he enjoys political influence or not.

In fact, while it is true that voodoo and its associated satanic rituals do enjoy significant influence in Haiti, it is equally true that the nation is populated by industrious and friendly people that are very family-oriented. Conversely, they have come to distrust politics because of the corruption that has dominated virtually every level of government.

Nevertheless, Chavannes, in his early fifties, was hopeful that he could motivate enough Christians to vote to swing the election his way. In fact, he has been characterized by at least one U.S. missionary as "the Billy Graham of Haiti."

Chavannes certainly has the credentials to support such a characterization. As the former leader of HAVIDEC (Haiti's Vision for the

Third Century), an evangelical social organization that was established to reach the nation with the Gospel as it began its third century of independence, and to motivate Christians to involve themselves in all aspects of Haitian life, including politics, Chavannes – who left the organization to run for president – has seen daily the challenges facing his people through God's call upon his life.

Out of the efforts of HAVIDEC came a political party, UNCRH, a French acronym for "National Christian Union for the Reconstruction of Haiti." Chavannes was elected as its leader – and by extension its presidential candidate – in January, 2005.

From that point, he began crisscrossing the nation, as well as the Atlantic Ocean, as he campaigned in remote areas here, as well as to the Haitian Diaspora, which is made up of about 2.5 million expatriated Haitians living in the United States, Canada, France, Africa and other nations. They were eligible to vote and send a documented $1 billion annually to friends, family and businesses back home. Additionally, it is anyone's guess as to how much cash is sent by family members back home without bank transfers.

He offered an ambitious agenda, but he is not a complete stranger to Haitian politics, as he served as vice president for 13 months at the beginning of the 1990's under President Ertha Fascal Trouyot. "During that time, the Lord allowed me to make a positive impact on leaders, as he allowed me to witness to many politicians and military leaders who accepted the Lord as their Savior," revealed Chavannes.

It is that pastor's heart that guided his platform. In short, though this last election led to temporary chaos until Preval was declared the winner, Chavannes believes Haiti is ripe for a Christian to be elected president at some point in the near future, which Chavannes insisted would be an embracing by Haitians of Jesus as the nation's Lord.

In fact, he referred to the first U.S. president as a model for the first point of his platform. "First of all, we need moral values. That is very much lacking. We have many leaders that are often corrupted. They enrich themselves and rob the people. Like George Washington said, a nation that is not guided by the moral principles of God has no guide at all."

He continued, "This is a democracy only on paper. Social justice is a major issue. We must decentralize. All the power is in the presidency and Port-au-Prince. Rural, remote areas are left behind."

As an example of how Haitians can govern themselves, he points to the small national police force. "We have only 4,000 police for a nation of 8.5 million people. Half of those are bodyguards for the big shots, and not helping the people at all. Yet, except for a few pockets, we can move about, live together without problems, even with no police presence."

It is those pockets of violence that must be immediately addressed before other points of his platform can be initiated, he acknowledged. "We can create jobs and encourage investment and tourism if we end the violence. It is a very beautiful country." He continued, "It is too bad the poverty and sense of oppression and lack of employment has led to violent actions."

So, beyond the belief that Christians must provide a moral example as leaders, he said, "The number one problem is security." The government must also be stabilized, he said, and jobs created because, "Poverty encourages violence."

The nation essentially has a year-round growing season, so production of agriculture must increase, he said, so the nation can import less food, saving extremely limited resources and providing desperately needed food for its population. So, working on infrastructure, such as irrigation, is critical, he said.

He also hopes to play a part in improving Haiti's standing in the international community. Chavannes acknowledged that will require a balancing act, as he does not wish Haiti to be subservient to other nations, but knows also that it must collaborate with them to help the Haitian people.

"Haiti cannot do well if it does not have good relations," he said. Chavannes said the nation must begin international cooperation with the Dominican Republic, the nation to the east that shares the island of Hispaniola with Haiti, and accounts for two-thirds of the land mass.

"We must try and see whether we can develop electricity. We share a big river that could accomplish that."

He continued, "Also, we have the United States only 600 miles away. We have to understand the role of the U.S. and smooth our relations, not see them as wanting to occupy and control Haiti. We must work together. The American people are inclined to help. We need the means without being subordinated."

He noted also that Haiti has a cultural connection to France, the nation that established Haiti as a colony. French is the official language spoken and is taught in school. He also spoke of establishing strong relations with Canada, where a large percentage of the Diaspora live, as well as Israel, Japan and even China. "We need a government that knows how to approach these nations as partners, to get collaboration but not submission."

Chavannes believes that Haiti has the culture and history that will demonstrate its value in the international community. "First of all, we have a wonderful culture. We are a very hospitable and industrious people." As examples, he pointed to the arts – in particular music and painting – and to the number of professionals the nation has produced. In the latter case, there are many Haitian doctors, but more live in Canada than in Haiti, he noted.

But to have accomplished all of that, he needed to convince Christians to register and vote. At the time, he said at least three obstacles stood in the way of that critical endeavor – violence in past elections, an under-funded and understaffed effort to register voters, and the belief held by many pastors that Christians should not engage in politics because it is so corrupt. He said flatly, "If the security is not resolved, we will have problems."

Some have even criticized the U.N., in particular for not securing Cite Soleil, allowing gangs to disrupt missionary activities, feeding programs, and other relief efforts. Chavannes acknowledged, "Everybody understands they are not efficient. Everybody knows they have not brought peace." Yet, insisted Chavannes, "I really believe there is some progress being made."

As for getting Christians involved in the election, he was hopeful. "The turnaround in the minds of the Christians about being involved is a pleasant surprise," said Chavannes. "If we all come out to vote, and vote in unison, we will win," he insisted. Undeniably, he does come from a region – the south – that could have propelled him into the presidency, for an estimated 57 percent of the residents there are Christians.

And, he said the new president must appeal to the Diaspora. "The leaders must acknowledge them. They have trade and skills we desperately need. If we can repatriate them, they are a rich source of ideas. Too often though, the leaders of this country have not utilized them and put their ideas on the shelf."

Though he faced many obstacles – the problems of Haiti itself, not to mention raising enough support for his campaign – he was determined. "I am in this endeavor to see if I can be of use to this country and use my testimony and Christian faith to influence our nation for good."

While he did not succeed in his run for president, few would doubt that he will continue to pursue this mission as a pastor and evangelical leader.

Church Tours

"Since you are eager to have spiritual gifts, try to excel in gifts that build up the church"
(1 Corinthians 14:12).

After leaving our meeting with Chavannes, Joseph said that we were going to go visit his father's church. Joseph's father has been deceased more than a decade, but it is the church he pastored, so that is how he refers to it.

So, through noisy, cluttered, dusty neighborhoods we ventured on this Friday morning. I expected – as would most members of a church in the United States – that our visit to the church would be a quiet one, to simply see the structure and perhaps enjoy some recollections of Joseph's.

However, when we arrived, we could not get into the church – not because it was locked, but because it was overflowing with congregants listening to the preaching of God's Word. Indeed, people were gathered outside the open windows, Bibles open, leaning in, straining to hear the preaching.

I squeezed in between a couple of folks to take a peak and behind the pulpit stood just one of many preachers that were on the stage for what I soon learned was a day-long revival service. Though I didn't understand the words, I got the message. People were clapping, raising their hands, and shouting in response. In short, they were eager to hear the Word – on Friday morning!

From there, we went to another church – the one pastored by Clerzius. It was empty, as he was busy running his factory this day, as you will read about next. Indeed, we visited the factory first, but the experience at the two churches this day – while strikingly different – were so similarly moving that the stories belong together.

Again, it was a bumpy, dusty and hot ride. Finally, we pulled up beside a small block building. I thought we had made a detour. Instead, we were at his church.

We went inside and Clerzius pointed proudly to the new construction, though it was incomplete. Some of the walls were now higher, part of the roof was concrete, though rusty metal still covered the front quarter or so of the church. Clerzius could not have been more proud than if it was a multi-million dollar, 15,000-seat mega-church so proudly hailed in the United States.

But his exuberance, while moving, was not the most inspiring aspect of the visit.

Shortly after we arrived, a young boy, perhaps 10 or so, appeared seemingly out of nowhere, sitting on a school desk near the back of the church (his face graces the cover and chapter title pages of this book). His eyes betrayed wisdom far beyond his years. He offered a broad grin, tempered by the pain of a life caused to mature much too quickly. With folded hands, he simply stared at me. I took his picture. I asked Joseph who he was. He didn't know. Neither did Clerzius. But they knew why he was there. The truck with the NDI logo on it, and the fact that this gray-haired, bearded white man had gotten out of the truck had made him eager to come visit. But not because he was expecting something; he never asked, never approached in such a manner. Rather, he knew that when someone from NDI was nearby, and when Clerzius was in his church, spiritual yearnings could be met. The eagerness of his eyes revealed it.

Providing Purpose
and Provision

"If a man will not work, he shall not eat"
(2 Thessalonians 3: 10b).

The Apostle Paul introduced the above precept by saying, "For even when we were with you, we gave you this rule" (2 Thessalonians 3: 10a). In the raising of my son and in my mentoring of many other young men, I have used this verse as a sledgehammer. After all, Paul said it was a rule. I despise slothfulness. It is because of how I was raised. It is because of what I learned as a Boy Scout and Explorer Scout. It is because I have worked for 35 years, with no sign of retirement in sight. It is because I live in the land of industry and opportunity and I truly believe that if a person wants to work, even if it means digging ditches, he can. For the record, I have dug ditches, quite recently in fact; I am not degrading this or any other physical labor. I am simply acknowledging it is backbreaking work with little recognition and even less pay.

But what about in Haiti? The unemployment rate there is roughly 85 percent. Clearly, the demand for jobs outnumbers the supply. Would it be fair to use the verse above like I do with the generation behind me?

Of course not. Yet, the truth of the Scripture is undeniable. It is Economics 101. Though bartering is not totally extinct, it is not the preferred method of exchange, because the trade requires that each party be able to provide a precise need for the other. So, to eat, one generally needs money. To have cash, one generally needs to work.

What does one do, however, when there is no work?

That is a question that haunted Clerzius.

So, he opened a sewing factory.

It is a block building on a narrow side street, dusty inside and out, not far from the airport. His company's name reflects his outlook – Best Products, Inc.

In it, his dozen or so employees make bags, backpacks and similar products on sewing machines that textile plants in the United States abandoned about the time our troops were returning home from the battlefields of Europe and the Pacific. He sews, he fixes.

His reason for operating a factory while he pastors a church and works as a dentist are simple. "It provides dignity. People must work to eat. They must not starve. They must not beg," he said as we sat cramped together in the front seat of the truck, riding from his factory to his church.

We were heading to the church because it had been recently renovated and I had agreed to accept his invitation to preach there the upcoming Sunday. But first, we visited the factory.

It was like walking into a cave. Clearly, the midday August sun in Port-au-Prince is high and bright. Still, adjusting our eyes after entering the building was not just because it was bright outside; the building is dimly lit. First, the building is a rental and some improvements are beyond his control. Plus, with the electric service being seemingly arbitrary, one must get accustomed to working through periods of blackouts, so spending very limited resources on expensive lighting would not be the most efficient use of his money.

The building is cavernous, with much unused space. In a corner room though, are a very industrious group of men and women. At the sewing machines sat the men, hands and feet moving at remarkable speed. The women, meanwhile, stocked the products. Clerzius moved to a table where finished products wait to be stacked, packed and shipped. He grabbed a blue bag with a large red cross on it. He had been blessed to receive a contract from the Red Cross.

He held it up, proudly pointing to the stitching and fabric.

He walked up and down the rows, checking the work, taking a moment to fix a snag here, another problem there. Indeed, when we walked in, he was sitting in the back corner, sewing.

It would seem he not only stitches together fabric; he does the same with lives – for he is a pastor that knows Scripture. A person that doesn't have work, can't eat. He can't – won't – accept that.

The Heart of an Evangelist

"But you, keep your head in all situations, endure hardship, do the work of an evangelist, discharge the duties of your ministry"
(2 Timothy 4: 5).

Jean Claude Jean-Baptiste (J.B.) is an energetic and intense man who is not easy to keep up with. Once one can get him to sit still for a moment though, this evangelist – who was overseeing construction of his new kindergarten on a dusty hilltop overlooking the city – was eager to sit and discuss his many endeavors at reaching this nation with the Gospel of Jesus Christ.

Sitting in a folding metal chair, in a yet-to-be-finished classroom for the school year that was to begin in just a month, J.B. spoke at a pace that exemplifies the tempo at which he moves.

Though he was at the new school, he preferred talking about the evangelical efforts he is leading, which began with a calling about 15 years ago. The kindergarten, he explained, is just part of that effort. "Haiti's problem is a heart problem. That's why we want to start with the little ones, to give them an education for a better Haiti."

He acknowledged, "It is difficult to help the older children." The reason, he said, is so many have already fallen into the clutches of the vices of the street. Hence, his school targets children of families that can't afford to pay for private education; public education exists, but its quality is of question and the Gospel is not shared in such schools.

A church in Marietta, Ga. has agreed to help cover the costs of the first two years of operation. The school is called Andrew Christian School, in honor of the church – St. Andrew United Methodist Church – that is helping them. After that, he expects the school to be too large, as the children age into higher grades. Though he planned to start with 30 children this year, he envisions the school eventually having 500 students, which would require that he find a new location.

For the moment though, his focus was evangelism.

In fact, just a week before he had concluded a crusade in the southern port city of Les Cayes, at which more than 600 hundred people accepted Christ. The year before, in the same location, more than 700 made the same decisions. Indeed, he holds the crusade there at the same time every year.

Such successes do not come without a price tag though, as it costs up to $40,000 to hold a crusade for several days. If he raises less, they cut programs or the length of the crusade so the quality of the effort does not suffer. Indeed, he calls the crusades the Movement for Efficient Evangelism (MEE).

If the testimonies he offered are any indication, the crusades are worth every dime.

He told the story of one convert from the 2004 crusade. "Last year, this man was the first converted. The man said he had a dream he was being chased by a man with a torch. The person said, 'If you don't want to get burned, go to Jesus Christ.' In this dream, he was told to go to the First Baptist Church and wait for missionaries."

The man, a voodoo priest, did. "The first thing when he woke up, he went to the church. There he stood, waiting, waiting, and waiting. Finally, our bus came in. He helped unload it. He told us about his dream. We prayed for him right then and there, and he accepted Christ." He continued, "Two other voodoo priests heard that and said they would not be at peace until they accepted God. They did."

That experience led him to share testimonies from the just recently completed crusade. As a result of what happened in 2004, many of the voodoo priests in the region joined forces to work against the crusade. So, they put together a potion made of powder and put it where the crusade was going to be. J.B. shared, "During a service, as we were praying, my wife was led by God's Spirit to go to a man and she laid hands on him. He said, 'Fire don't get me!' He added, 'Please forgive me. I was paid. I realize God is more powerful.' He asked forgiveness and accepted Jesus."

J.B. added, "Those are just two testimonies of many of the great works God is doing."

Such testimonies are all the more reason he wants to expand to at least 10 crusades a year – one in each department of Haiti (similar to U.S. states). "We have to preach the Gospel in each of those 10 departments," insisted J.B. But his vision does not stop there. "After that, we will be traveling to other countries to preach the Gospel."

Such a claim might seem presumptuous – if not preposterous – considering that J.B. lacks the funds now to get to more than one or two sections of Haiti. Yet, a visit to the Christian churches here reveals a passion for Christ rarely seen in the United States anymore. For instance, Clerzius holds church services in the small, cinder-block building of a back alley, with only a partial roof and open sides. Yet, 150 or so people crowd into the church – no bigger than most Sunday school classrooms in U.S. churches – at 7 a.m. In fact, wherever evangelicals are meeting, the churches are reminiscent of the biblical accounts of first century churches, with people crowding around doors and windows to hear the preaching.

So clearly, Haitians are eager to hear the Gospel.

Not surprising then, J.B. admitted, "What we're hoping to do is find a supporter for each crusade." Each is designed to include programs for men, women and children, but are trimmed back, depending upon resources. He explained, "We have the structure and personnel. It is the lack of funds that limit us."

Basing his model on the methods used by the Billy Graham Evangelistic Association, J.B. partners with local pastors, who then agree to disciple those who accept Christ. He said that he would like to set up a program for the new converts, but realizes it is not practical now.

Nothing seems to dampen his passion, though. He disappeared for a moment to return with an EvangeCube, an unfolding square puzzle, distributed by E3 Resources in Franklin, Tenn. In it is the entire plan of salvation. It is one of his most effective tools for sharing the Gospel, he says.

A telling example of his zeal is the story of his first crusade, at Port-au-Prince, in 1997. Scheduled about the same time as his wedding, he was short on funds. Even though he had contacted 40 pastors to solicit their support, only two responded. So, he asked his future bride, "Would you agree to invest our wedding money into the crusade? She responded, 'If it is for God, yes.' Even so, every one that was at our wedding said it was one of the most beautiful that they had seen."

He added simply, "God does provide."

Transformed

"Do not conform any longer to the pattern of this world, but be transformed by the renewing of your mind"

(Romans 12:2a).

More and more, Robbie's promise that I would be transformed by my visit was happening. The people I had interviewed, visited and seen had indeed left me broken. Chavannes, willing to risk his very life to seek the presidency; the people filling Joseph's church to overflowing to hear the Word of God preached; Clerzius, operating a factory, serving as a dentist and pastoring a church; J.B, traveling the country to share the Gospel and building a school to provide a hope and a future; and finally, the young boy who had eased into Clerzius' church, just to be near us.

All were eager to share and hear the Gospel.

At this point, while I was still being astonished, I was no longer being surprised by God's moving, by His going before us, by His humbling of my soul and spirit. So, when I had read my journal and Bible that morning, I not only reflected upon the day before, I also eagerly anticipated how what I read that morning would prove to be so meaningful by the end of the day.

In short, by this point, the studies had begun to not only allow me to capture the experiences the day before; they also were harbingers of events and experiences to follow.

Certainly, such was the case from this day's study from the "Utmost" study, "The Baffling Call of God." The first phrase I underlined was, "Jesus Christ called his disciples to see Him put to death; He led every one of them to the place where their hearts were broken." I thought this phrase applied to the day before. It did. But, with the benefit of hindsight, I can see that the Lord was preparing me for what this day would hold.

The study continued, "There comes the baffling call of God in our lives also. The call of God can never be stated explicitly; it's implicit. The call of God is like the call of the sea, no one hears it but the one who has the nature of the sea in him." At this point, I scribbled in the side, "Like the last year." It continued, "It cannot be stated definitely what the call of God is to, because His call is to be in comradeship with Himself for His own purposes, and the test is to believe that God knows what He is after. The things that happen do not happen by chance, they happen entirely in the decree of God. God is working out His purposes."

Astonished, I was unable to respond in writing. Even when I returned from Haiti, I was completely puzzled. I could not, for the life of me, figure out what the experience was about. I constantly felt – during the trip and afterward – overwhelmed. It took a full five or six months after my return from Haiti to understand one purpose of the experience – to share how God does use the meek of the world to humble us – to teach us to be His bond-slaves.

So, I struggled for a season as to what God would have me to learn. The final entry I underlined that day offers a clue. "A Christian is one who trusts the wits and the wisdom of God, and not his own wits. If we have a purpose of our own, it destroys the simplicity and the leisureliness which ought to characterize the children of God."

I was at my wits end this day, and for weeks – months – thereafter. And, that is exactly where God wanted me.

My entry in the journal that day seems trite compared to what I have learned since that day. I wrote, "Jesus has led me to a point where my heart is broken – repeatedly. This visit to Haiti is indeed heart-wrenching. The nation is impoverished – economically, politically and spiritually." Little did I know that when I wrote that, that I would look back and realize how impoverished I was – spiritually. It was only through my broken heart that Jesus could teach me that.

Day 4: Saturday, August 6

Comfort and Confidence

Looking for My Name

"Nothing impure will ever enter it, nor will anyone who does what is shameful or deceitful, but only those whose names are written in the Lamb's book of life"

(Revelation 21:27).

Saturday was a day of rest and reflection. I knew I had much to write, but I knew I had the full day to do it, with the appointment book clear.

The roosters would not allow me to sleep in; however, I enjoyed several leisurely cups of coffee and allowed myself more time to study from my Bible and the "Utmost for His Highest" journal, given to me by my family on Father's Day – a simple, but powerful gift that I have come to expect each year so that I can reflect back and track each year of my life's journey. That I get it on Father's Day is particularly poignant for many reasons. One is obvious – it is a gift from my wife and children. But it is also appropriate, for it is an accounting of my journey with our heavenly Father.

Saturday, then, because it was free of appointments, and also because it was the halfway point of the trip, seemed like an appropriate time to begin writing that which was more reflective than reporting. Sitting on the front porch, overlooking the alley, I allowed my mind to drift backwards over the last few days. I wasn't sure where the musings would take me. As is the often the case though, when I have the leisure of not having to meet deadline pressures, a parable – a metaphor – from the first moments of the journey developed.

It was of my first moments in Haiti.

As I exited the airport terminal there, I was entering into a land that I had never before visited. So, I was counting upon others to do the advance work and make preparations for me so that when I arrived, I would be welcome and safe.

As I looked at the U.N. troops with their imposing guns, and looked out into a sea of strange faces, I was very much hoping to see my name on a piece of paper, knowing that the person holding it – whom I had never met – would be guiding me to safety through the crowd and to the guest house. I did not know where I was going, so I did not know the way.

I was hopeful that all the proper arrangements had been made. While I had complete confidence in those responsible, I know also that humans are not infallible and that lines of communications can break down, so I was admittedly a bit apprehensive when at first, I saw nobody coming forward with a piece of paper with my name on it.

But then he appeared. I was quite relieved, as you can imagine.

Though I was not certain that my companion would greet me, I have no such fear about whether or not, when I exit this life, someone will be waiting on me with my name in their book. For Jesus did the advance work and made preparations for me, so that when I arrive, I will be welcomed. Through His death on the cross, He defeated sin. Through His resurrection, He defeated death. When I put my trust in Him as my Lord and Savior, my name was written in the Lamb's book of life.

Just as I had only one person at the airport that could deliver me to safety, people have only one connection with God that can deliver us to safety – Jesus Christ. Scripture reports, "Thomas (an apostle of the Lord) said to him, 'Lord, we don't know where you are going, so how can we know the way?' Jesus answered, 'I am the way and the truth and the life. No one comes to the Father except through me' " (John 14:5-6 NIV).

So, I don't have to be apprehensive about leaving this life. I won't have to be looking for my name. It is already there, for Scripture promises it. I know that when I exit this planet, Jesus will pull me to safety.

If you do not share that confidence, I invite you to read the Bible for yourself and earnestly ask that God will reveal His truths to you, including how to be sure you will see your name on paper when you exit this life.

He wants your name in that book, so He will eagerly accept you – but only if you put your faith in Jesus.

Looking for Me

"There is no speech or language where their voice is not heard"

(Psalm 19: 3).

Ronald Frasius Romeus had been told by Wes than an American Christian journalist was staying at Providence House. Ronald is the overseer of a home for young Haitian men in their teens and twenties, young men that others have abandoned. Collectively, they are known as the Haitian Christian Youth (HCY). I met them on my last night in Haiti, so you will read about them later. But Wes, who formed HCY, knew that Ronald is up to much more than just being the mentor for these young men, a fulltime job in itself. So, he suggested that Ronald pay me a visit.

However, Wes did not tell me to expect Ronald. They had connected by email after my arrival in Port-au-Prince; the hectic schedule since I first stepped foot on the tarmac had not given Wes time to alert me to Ronald's visit.

There was another problem as well. Joseph had left the guest house for the day to take care of some personal responsibilities, so I had no translator. Ronald spoke English just barely better than I speak French, which is to say not at all.

Taking a peak at the courtyard while taking a break from writing, I saw a young man sitting in the courtyard of the guest house. This was not unusual, as visitors were not uncommon. It did not occur to me that the man was looking for me. Out of curiosity, I meandered into the courtyard and nodded at the young man who smiled pleasantly. I started to go back into the house when he said one of the few English phrases he knew – "Wes Morgan."

I had learned that his name had become like a secret password used to break the language barrier. So, I sat at the table this young man was leaning on and extended my hand. He asked, "Michael?"

I replied, "Yes."

He again said, "Wes."

It was the beginning of a two hour "conversation" carried out on a notepad. As it turned out, he could write some English. After about 20 or 30 minutes of trying to understand one another until we both were frustrated, Ronald motioned with his hand as if he was writing. So, I went up to my bedroom and returned with a notebook and pen.

It was the beginning of a sweet exchange. Ronald wanted me to know about his church and his school, as well as HCY. After providing basic contact information, he wrote about his priorities in life.

First was God – the name of his church. It is Beraca Baptist Christian Church.

Next, was the name of his wife – Marie.

Next, the children he serves – the name of his new school, Beraca Institution.

Regarding the school, he noted that he is the headmaster – "Program Director General," the Haitian equivalent of CEO. His wife serves as academic director and the school also has a pedagogic director. He anticipated hiring eight professors – an increase of two from the year before – for the academic year, which began in September. He also noted the meager salaries for which the teachers are willing to work – between about $40 and $120 U.S. per month, depending upon the position. Still, he wrote, even that was more than he had been able to raise.

He invited me to come visit his new school, which I agreed to do, contingent upon Joseph's agreement. (We did, so you will read about that a little later).

He also wrote "HCY" on the paper, and I agreed to find a way to meet these young men he was so concerned about.

As the sun began to set, I became concerned for his safety, as being out after dark in Port-au-Prince is not advisable. The "bad guys" threaten the day; they rule the night. So, I pointed to the lowering sun and said, "Marie" while motioning my hands as if I was steering a car. He nodded that he understood, but held up his hand to indicate there was something more I needed to know.

He placed the pen on the pad and gently pushed it back to me. He placed his hands over his chest and shook his head from side-to-side. "Non" he said simply. Then, he pointed to the sky and said, "For Jesus." I understood. He had shared all of this, not for his glory, but for that of the Lord's.

He then added, in two of the few English phrases he had come to learn, "I love you. I am blessed."

No, I thought. To know that Ronald not only does not know where the funding for his church, school and HCY will come from, but literally lives day-to-day counting upon the Lord for his own and his family's provision, yet is so focused on ministry, and has an eternal smile on his face, it was I that was blessed.

After Ronald left, I went back upstairs, sat at the desk, pointed the fan at the chair, opened my Bible, and prepared my message for the following morning. I already knew what I was going to say. It was the revelation that had come to me on the mountaintop on our "sightseeing" trip Thursday afternoon.

I wanted to match Scripture with the message however, to ensure that my message was biblically sound, and after affirming that, to have verses that would support my illustrations. I finished and folded my sheet of notebook paper into the page I would first reference.

A few moments later, Joseph returned. I told him about Ronald and he said that we should have time to see him on Monday. I then excitedly shared with him that I had completed the preparation for my message the next morning. He smiled and said simply, "Good." I excused myself for a moment and told him I'd be right back. I went upstairs, grabbed my Bible and came back downstairs with the notes. I held them before him and asked, "Would you look at these please." He just looked at me. I continued, "I want to make sure I'm not going to say anything that is culturally insensitive. Plus, since you are going to translate, I thought you might want to see them."

He looked almost perplexed. "I do not check behind the Holy Spirit," he said. "You've told me God has given you the message. Who am I to question that?"

A Vital Purpose

*"So we say with confidence, 'The Lord is my helper;
I will not be afraid. What can man do to me?'"*
                                                (Hebrews 13:6).

Because of the leisurely pace of the day, compared at least, to the balance of the trip, my written reflections in my journal and Bible for Saturday were not as extensive as other days, as the section above, "Looking for My Name," was the primary writing response to the thoughts and prayers I had on Saturday.

Still, that morning, Chambers' study, "The Cross in Prayer," certainly contributed to my thinking for the rest of the day, for I considered how the Haitians I had met up to then had demonstrated their absolute devotion to the truths represented and made possible by the cross. And, as the day wore on and I prepared for the opportunity to preach the next morning, my thoughts naturally turned to the central symbol and cause for our faith – the cross of Calvary.

The first passage I underlined that day was, "The idea of prayer is not in order to get answers from God; prayer is perfect and complete oneness with God." Before I left for Haiti, I asked numerous people to pray for me while there. The observation by Chambers affirmed what I was beginning to grasp – that I was learning, from the meekest of people, to be a bond-slave of Christ, to accept the inconceivable truth of the incarnation. Prayer – not only my own, which daily included, "OK, God. What in the world is going on here?" – but also intercessory prayers by others were, in my mind, unquestionably drawing me closer to God.

Next I underlined, "We are not here to prove God answers prayer; we are here to be living monuments of God's grace." He was addressing the nature of God and our relationship with Him. And, the example that our relationship and faith walk sets for others. Again, as I applied this observation to those I had met in Haiti, it was true. Like the song, "One Day at a Time," these brothers and sisters were wholly dependent upon God's provision – one day at a time. That their faith seemed to strengthen with each day, with each set of trying circumstances, with an increasing measure as uncertainty dominated their daily lives, proved the claim made by Chambers. They are, literally, *living* monuments to God's grace. Despite their circumstances, they live each day fully, as if it might be their last. They depend entirely upon God. That they rise up each morning, that they persevere – despite trials of many kinds – is a testimony to God's grace.

Finally, I underlined, "Has our Lord's vicarious life become your vital life?" I circled the word vital.

In response, I entered into the journal, "While it would be folly for me to think I've arrived, it is true that this trip to Haiti makes me more alive – vital – than ever. In fact, the other morning I caught myself praying for finances so that I could be 'free.' I stopped myself (or the Holy Spirit did) in mid-sentence. If these folks – who are truly impoverished – can rely upon God daily, such a prayer is selfish. I do find myself just talking, praying and listening to God for His will. It is amazing how such a prayer life provides complete peace."

Appropriately, it was such early day musings that led me to have my mind clear enough to grab hold of the truth that, when I die, I will not have to experience anxiety looking for my name.

Saturday, indeed, was a day of comfort and confidence.

Day 5: Sunday, August 7

Exhausted but Encouraged

The Haiti High

*"Since an overseer is entrusted with God's work...
he must hold firmly to the trustworthy message as it
has been taught, so that he can encourage others by
sound doctrine and refute those who oppose it"*
                                    (Titus 1: 7a, 9).

I am not an ordained minister, but God has allowed me numerous opportunities to preach the Gospel. Each opportunity has been a tremendous honor, for to share God's Word is a solemn stewardship responsibility.

In fact, I am very hesitant to stand behind a pulpit, for I am all too aware of my own failings, and know that God has entrusted teachers of His Word with an awesome responsibility and that the requirements expected of such a teacher are high indeed. Even when my own pastor allows me to share just a word or two with our congregation, I thank him and commit the opportunity to serious prayer, for I believe that stewardship precepts teach that a pastor that surrenders his pulpit to another will be held accountable by God for what that person says.

This morning, in the most humble of surroundings, I was honored again to preach the story of Jesus. During my first evening in Haiti, when Clerzius came to Providence House, he asked me, as we finished our visit, if I would preach at his church.

I told him I would pray about it. Then the next day, when Joseph and Stanley took me to the mountaintop on our sightseeing tour and I was amazed at the level of poverty and the lack of commerce, I knew that God had answered affirmatively my prayer as to whether or not I was to accept Clerzius' offer. Indeed, I was excited when Joseph told me on Friday morning that we would be visiting Clerzius's factory. I couldn't wait to tell him that God had provided a message so that I could accept his offer.

During the ride from the factory to the church he leads, I told him I would be honored to fulfill his request.

But I had no idea how honored.

Sunday morning in Port-au-Prince is quiet, just as it is in the United States. But it starts much earlier. As Joseph and I opened the gate of the guest house that morning to pull the truck out, it was about 6:45. I expected to see an empty alleyway. Instead, I was immediately greeted with a friendly nod from a mother and her child – dressed in their finest clothes and Bibles in hand. The child looked as if she was going to an Easter service, in her white shoes and a yellow and lavender hat with flowers. On our way to the church, every alley and every street was full of people walking briskly, dressed unlike I had seen people attired during the week, most with Bibles in their hands.

They were headed to church. Saturday night belongs to the ruffians, but Sunday morning belongs to the saints.

After about a 15-minute bumpy ride, we had arrived at the church we had visited on Friday. On that first visit, I would not have recognized it as a church from the outside.

On Friday, it looked like an abandoned building or perhaps a storage facility. Yet, this morning, as Joseph and I entered, there were already about 150 or so people crowded into the church – no bigger than most Sunday school classrooms in American churches – at 7 a.m. In fact, wherever Christians meet in Port-au-Prince, the churches are reminiscent of the biblical accounts of first century churches, with people crowding around doors and windows to hear the preaching.

Crowded, but segregated by Sunday school classes – one for new converts, one for women and one for men – the church members listened attentively to their teachers and answered questions, despite having to compete with one another to hear. The classes lasted about 45 minutes. As they closed, each group stood and recited memory verses in unison. First the new converts, then the women, then the men.

We all then exited the building. The choir needed to sit where the new converts class had been sitting, but the church was literally too small for everyone to get rearranged while in the building, so everyone moved outside. The choir went in first, followed by the women, and then the men. The waiting provided an opportunity for a time of impromptu fellowship, characterized by smiling and animated conversations.

Finally, Clerzius, Joseph, the elders and I entered the church to sit near the altar and pulpit.

Clerzius opened his Bible and Joseph told me he was reading from Psalm 96. I opened my Bible; though I didn't understand the Creole in which Clerzius was speaking, it didn't matter. God's Spirit touched my heart as I read the words while tuning in to Clerzius's inflection and tone.

Then, the choir stood to sing. About 40-strong, led by their director who also played the piano, they sang crisply and beautifully a song that immediately recognized from the tune – "Rock of Ages."

Clerzius then introduced me and I again heard that password that I had heard from Ronald the night before – Wes Morgan. Wes, he was telling them, has sent me to Haiti. They applauded. Joseph shared with me that he was explaining that he had asked me to preach, that I told him I would pray about it, explained how I had come to conclude, from my visit to the mountaintop that I was to preach, and surrendered the pulpit to me.

I don't know that I have ever felt so inadequate. I quietly and quickly muttered to myself, "Lord, let the meditations of my heart and the words of my lips please you and make sense."

Teaming with Joseph, I shared Scripture from Genesis and Revelation, as well as other books.

I "preached" to them what I suspected they already knew – that Haiti's problems are spiritual. All that I could do was speak from my own experiences – growing up in the United States and looking at Haiti through the lens that such a life and a biblical worldview offered. I spoke to them of their obvious industriousness. I acknowledged that I knew that Haiti, when it declared its independence more than 200 years ago, pledged its national soul to the devil, and was still paying for that decision. I noted that it seemed that the United States, in many ways, had now done the same. I shared that from the mountaintop, I was awestruck by the city's beautiful mountains and seaport, but perplexed by its lack of commerce. I explained how I had concluded that these human and natural resources were largely going to waste because of Haiti's spiritual darkness.

But I said they had the Light, that they were the light for their nation. I told them they held the only hope for Haiti – Jesus Christ. I concluded by encouraging them, regardless of their circumstances, to hold fast to that truth and to never give up. I acknowledged there might be people there that didn't have this hope, and if so, to seek out the pastor, an elder or a friend that had brought them, so that they, too, could have the only hope that is lasting.

Recognizing that I was truly in the presence of surrendered Christians, I asked them to pray for my family.

All of this I did in a church still not completely built, with a rusty tin roof, with walls that didn't reach the ceiling. And I was talking to them about hope.

Their mere presence seemed to make my message redundant. But it was the message that God had given me, that Joseph the night before did not question, that he translated patiently and with the same enthusiasm with which I delivered it.

I sat down, wondering what they thought of this U.S. journalist that their beloved friend Wes had sent to them. I wondered why God had blessed me so. I wondered why, of all the people on the planet, God had chosen me to be at this spot, at this time.

All that I could discern was that God was trying to teach me. I knew, without a doubt, He loved me. Why else would He have allowed me to be in the presence of such faithful saints?

As these questions were racing around my head, Clerzius and others prepared bread and juice, and we joined together to remember our Lord.

Clerzius stood back up and made a few announcements. The service closed with the choir standing, singing a tune that was again instantly recognizable – "The Battle Hymn of the Republic." Though I did not understand the language, I have never been so moved by its singing.

Most touching though was the way they responded for the request from me to pray for my family. All stood, and for several minutes, in a language that I could not interpret – but I did understand – the entire church prayed as I had asked.

Afterwards, several people said they were blessed. Again, I heard, "Thank you." "I love you." "God bless you." There were no language barriers then.

That, I am told, is the Haiti High. If God allows, I'll be back for more, for it is addicting.

A Living Sacrifice

"Therefore, I urge you brothers, in view of God's mercy, to offer your bodies as living sacrifices, holy and pleasing to God – this is your spiritual act of worship"

(Romans 12:1).

The balance of Sunday was much like Saturday. As God intended, it was a day of rest. Joseph offered me some options, including visiting a couple of people, but I decided to ask that we stay at the guest house. I still had writing I was behind on, and my body needed the rest. I knew one more day of not bouncing around in the truck – especially when I considered the agenda for the next two days and my need to catch up on my writing – was the wisest choice.

I awoke exhausted. I knew the cold shower was necessary, but I knew also that a putting on a shirt and tie in the stifling humidity would have me needing another shower before we even left for church. In short, when I got out of the bed Sunday, I was simultaneously excited and lethargic. I was excited about worshipping in Clerzius' church, with his congregation. I was honored and enthused that I would be preaching, and I was astonished at the message that God had given me throughout the previous three days.

Yet, I still had to force myself to sit up in the bed, to place my feet on the floor, and to trek across the commons area to the bathroom. "Rest," I thought. "I just need rest."

I lifted a short prayer. "Stamina, Lord. I need stamina." Immediately, I recalled, "Come to me, all you who are weary and burdened, and I will give you rest" (Matthew 11:28). I then recalled the study from the day before. God is demonstrating his grace through this answered prayer, I thought. Yes, my body was worn out, but Jesus would provide. Instantly, I knew it was His grace I was experiencing, for there was nothing else I could draw upon for strength.

Once ready, I still had 45 minutes before the time Joseph said we needed to leave. It was too early for breakfast, so I grabbed my "Utmost" and my Bible and sat at my favorite spot, at the top of the stairs.

It was only a matter of seconds before I knew God was going to be speaking to be me clearly through the study. Though they are not designed to fall on a specific day of the week – they go by date, regardless of what day that might be – the study for this day was, "Prayer in the Father's House."

The Scripture verse for the study was "Wist ye not that I must be in My Father's house!" (Luke 2:49 RV). I immediately circled it. I thought of my fatigue and was ashamed for even thinking about it. I was to be at church. A few tired bones were no excuse for not getting up.

Reading on, I underlined, "Do I look upon life as being in my Father's house? Is the Son of God living in His Father's house in me?" Translated: we make our bodies a living sacrifice – no matter how tired they are – so God can use them as His dwelling, for His purposes.

The next sentence noted, "The abiding Reality in God, and His order comes through the moments." What moments, I wondered, was I to have this day to experience the reality of God? A little further down the page, I underlined, "I must be about My Father's business." Two thoughts crossed my mind – that I was to be obedient to God and share what he had placed in my heart; and, I was to make my body available to Him for His business.

Also in the passage was this observation, "Narrow it down to your individual circumstances – are you so identified with the Lord's life that you are simply a child of God, continually talking to Him, realizing that all things come from His hands?" I admitted to myself that I had not been, but that Haitian Christians were demonstrating this to me.

Finally, I underlined, "Let Him have His way, keep in perfect union with Him." I meditated upon this. It was a scary thought. Our free will can keep us from having His way with us. I was thankful that I had already met so many examples of people that took this seriously. Their examples – their living sacrifices – were challenging me to heed this call.

After reading Chambers' entry, I responded, "A good message for this morning, for I am exhausted, sore and feeling a little poorly. This heat, work here has worn me down. Yet, I prepare to go to your church. So, I pray for strength. I pray that God uses me this morning to encourage and edify my Haitian brothers and sisters, and if necessary, lead unbelievers to Christ. Amen."

Immediately after the service, which you've read about above, I returned and humbly wrote, with an arrow pointing from that last sentence into blank space left on the page, "It was I that was encouraged!"

Day 6: Monday, August 8

Reflecting the Affliction of Christ

Rehabilitating the Heart

*"Born with heaven in their eyes/God sent, innocent/
The promise of life/Born into this mess we've made/
Holding the future/And hope of better days/Cause
there is nothing more beautiful and wild/Than the
dreams that grow in the heart of every child."(Lyrics
from Kathy Mattea's "They Are The Roses," the title
track on her album "Roses," penned by Randy Van
Warmer, Tim Schoepf and Paul Jenkins).*

Jehu Metellus could be living a comfortable, quiet life, serving as a
church pastor in Canada or the United States, where he has many
friends and associates. Instead, this man in his early fifties spends
all of his days in his native country raising about two dozen boys
– all rescued from the hard streets of Haiti's capital and surrounding
towns.

Jehu, whose home, the Rehabilitation Center of Special Education
(CRES, the acronym for the French pronunciation) houses boys
ranging from age two to 18, said his vision – which he developed
while doing graduate work in psychology – is simple. All he wants,
he said, "Is to see the boys live well."

There is only one such way to accomplish such a daunting task,
he insisted. "Our mission is to lead the children to Jesus Christ."

He continued, "We do this by educating them spiritually, evan-
gelically, and socially so that they know they are human and are able

to respect themselves and others. This way, they can be a good role model for society, despite their backgrounds."

Considering some of the stories he told, such a result would seem miraculous. One boy, only two-years-old, was rescued from sure death, as he was the planned sacrifice for a voodoo ritual. The child was so totally abandoned that Jehu named him. Another was going to be traded for a television set. He added, "They all have a story like that."

With such backgrounds, there is a long way to go before they are what Jehu envisions they will be. Indeed, their first three months here is spent in "Awakening Training," in which Jehu explained they are taught, "They need to change the mindset gained from being in the street." He said they need to be taught they are human, to know how to respond to people, and basic things, like not to dump trash in the street and not to urinate just anywhere.

"We must show them a better life so they can adjust to the program," he said. "We are reforming delinquent people. We are striving to produce people that know the norms, values and rules of godly behavior."

Why accept such a challenge? Simply stated, God called him to it, he said, beginning with planting the idea after his ordination as a pastor in 1992. He decided to further his education, and as he studied psychology his first year, the idea came to him. "Pastors only focus on a certain kind of people and forget about the children on the street," argued Jehu. "This idea continued to haunt me." So, he did his thesis on street children, leading him to conclude, "If we don't take care of the children now, the future is at grave risk. Not only those children that go to school can influence society, but street children can influence it as well."

While Port-au-Prince does have its share of bright spots – in particular friendly, warm people, a Caribbean port, beautiful mountains and a fertile valley – it is also filthy, corrupt and disease-ridden, lending credence to Jehu's argument.

The city offers a constant assault on the senses. Smoke from burning trash – even on the sidewalks of the city's busiest thoroughfare – combines with black smoke from cars and trucks unregulated by emission standards and a gray dust from the broken streets to constantly burn the nostrils. Cars, buses and trucks are abandoned in the middle of busy roadways and back alleys, some abandoned so long that they are but mere rusted-out shells. Mosquitoes breed in standing brown water, creeks have beds composed more of trash than rocks, and constantly barking dogs with ribs showing roam without constraint. Pigs, goats and chickens wander through the trash.

In the midst of it all are thousands of abandoned children, many of them AIDS orphans, left to fend for themselves by families too poor to provide even the most basic necessities of life, or simply refusing to honor their responsibilities.

That is where Jehu comes in, though he acknowledged it took awhile for the call that was haunting him to become reality. A former professor asked him in 2001 what his vision was. He answered, "I don't want a church. I feel my calling is in helping children."

To get help in fulfilling his vision, in 2001 he went to a pastor whose church was near some land that Jehu could rent. If he could rent that land, thought Jehu, he could make his dream a reality – particularly because he wanted the boys to be close to a church. So, he asked the pastor if he would collaborate with him in renting the land.

The initial contact did not go well. "I told the pastor of my vision and he said, 'I have good news. There is land in Cite Soleil. It is one hectare. We'll purchase it.'" However, Jehu was not interested, for it did not match his vision and Cite Soleil is not a place for young boys.

Jehu told the pastor he would be more than willing to rescue boys from the streets there, but not operate there. It is simply too dangerous. So, the pastor refused to help – at first. Jehu recalled, "When the pastor went to bed that night, he could not sleep, because God was dealing with his conscience. He came back the next day and said, 'I apologize. I told a friend I would not help them because he would not do things my way. I am sorry. I will help.' He agreed to pay the first six months rent on the house." That was $3,000. Another $3,000 came from the former professor.

"I trusted that the Lord would make a way. So indeed, he did," offered Jehu.

Since then, NDI has partnered with Jehu, providing CRES with various supplies, including a truck, computer, a cell phone and other necessities. The home still needs a generator and inverter, essential equipment until the unpredictable electrical service is improved.

What it lacks in equipment and supplies, however, is made up in love. Two days a week are spent on Bible study and the remainder of the week is devoted to other academic lessons. Perhaps the most telling tribute to Jehu's work was the mini-concert offered by two boys, each who played a brief tune on their flutes. As one watched and listened to the boys, it did, indeed, seem miraculous that they would be playing lovely music, when not too long ago they were hustling on the streets just to survive.

The turnaround is easily explained, Jehu said. "We have love for them in our hearts, but they must be disciplined, just as Jesus wants us to follow the right path. If not, we'll be chastised."

Working with just a staff of six and himself, Jehu has grand visions for the future. His objective is to build a facility large enough to hold 200-300 children. Such a vision is indeed God-sized, as land here is quite expensive, as are building costs. But, in a town about 45 minutes from Port-au-Prince, Jehu has purchased 2 hectares of land for $250,000 Haitian gourds (a little over $30,000 U.S.) A government grant provided $100,000 and he still owes the balance.

They have started building a wall on the land. He explained, "In Haiti, when you purchase land, you have to show your presence, or others will move in. The way you do it is wall it in." Indeed, walled-in empty lots dot the hillsides here, as landowners – despite having deeds – must "claim" the land or end up fighting for it.

His plan is to build in phases. He first intends to build a dorm, then the school, then a bakery, and finally a church. He said the church comes last because he wants the bakery so the ministry can help support itself, and because worship can be held in other buildings. But eventually the church would house an auditorium, dining room and sanctuary.

Though he does not want to lead a church, Jehu feels the call of a pastor. "Spiritually, they have a soul that needs saved. As a pastor, it is my duty to put them on the right path. Like Jesus said, let the children come to me. It is a privilege to lead them to Christ and to be a positive influence on society as well."

Ronald's Heart

"Let the little children come to me, and do not hinder them, for the kingdom of God belongs to such as these"

(Mark 10:14).

After leaving the CRES home and grabbing a sandwich at Providence House (even though they insist lunch is not part of the arrangement), we headed to Ronald's school. Again, it was a trip of bumps and sharp, narrow turns that took us to a neighborhood packed with small concrete shanties. We negotiated a narrow passageway, climbed and then descended a set of stairs and finally came through a narrow door.

Inside was a remodeled room with brand new chairs, arranged in anticipation of the arrival of students in a few weeks. Ronald invited us into his small office, which afforded him a stunning view of the city below and the port in the distance, though it was barely discernable because of the haze from the smog.

He offered us each a Coke, and we settled in to talk about his vision for the children of his neighborhood and his plans to implement it.

He explained how he had decided to begin the school, and to be a pastor. "I used to work with a pastor in Cabaret. He had a school there." With always tight finances, after three months, circumstances prevented the two from continuing their work together. Ronald admitted he was crushed. "I had nothing to do. My wife and I prayed and cried before the Lord." As a result of the prayer, he developed a vision. God, he believed, was leading him to hold a crusade in this neighborhood of Port-au-Prince, Delmas 40.

"We did," he offered simply. That was 2001. From that, he planted a church that included 52 children. "That's how we started our ministry. As we were teaching the children, God brought more, including adults. Spiritually, the work was growing, but without a building. So we prayed. We met our brother Wes Morgan. Through him, we were able to get this building."

Ronald explained that he met Wes at a guest house where he was staying. They both slept in the same wing of the home. "The last day of the seminar, they had preached a message that really troubled me. The message was that pastors and leaders should stop begging for help and trust in the Lord. To beg is to diminish the Lord."

So, offered Ronald, he prayed, "God, you know I have needs. I do not want to be a beggar to do your work. I know you can make a way!" He continued, "The next morning, Wes pulled at my shirt. That's how he introduced himself. We started talking about our work. He said he would help get us started with the first year's rent." Wes was pleased with Ronald's stewardship and results of the limited resources, so he agreed to help with two more years of rent.

"Because Wes Morgan helped, we are able to have this place here." Ronald acknowledged, softly, that Wes also helped him and his wife with their rent and also helped him by employing him as the director of the Haitian Christian Youth.

He added, "I believe that was a blessed appointment."

The school, which is called Mixed Institution Bereca, is based upon the belief that by providing for "the social aspect" – education and at least one meal a day – Ronald and the other teachers will earn the right to share the Gospel. At the time of our meeting, Ronald had not been able to pay the teachers their full salaries for the previous school year, yet all planned to return. "We still continue to trust the Lord for the money," he said. "We have a big vision, not only for the school, but we have long term goals to have a larger place for a church and the school."

He also hopes to have a feeding program for children, to provide shelter for the disabled, to provide for widows, to open a clinic, to start an orphanage for street children, and to grow his primary school to include a secondary and vocational school as well. "We believe from what God has done so far for us, that these things will happen. With prayer, anything is possible."

He acknowledged these are big dreams, but insisted that when these dreams are accomplished, only God can receive the glory. Until then, he is content with teaching children, because he knows how important an education is for them. "We have so much violence. Community life requires education. This has been lacking. That is because the parents can't afford the expenditure. That is why our church has opened this school. The young people will be better sociable beings. In that way, we are able to better serve the Haitian community in general and that of Delmas in particular."

He concluded, "It is not a secret for anybody that the investment in the social life allows us to share the hope that is in our Lord Jesus Christ." While this is the ultimate hope, Ronald also insists that reducing illiteracy will improve the neighborhood, reduce violence and increase the economic vitality of his neighborhood. Then, he said, the claims made about Jesus will be proven true.

Haitian Christian Youth

"Train a child in the way he should go, and when he is old he will not turn from it"

(Proverbs 22:6).

They are Haiti's future.

Yet, the stories of their pasts are enough to break one's heart. That they offer hope for the future, that they do indeed believe in themselves enough to actually speak of not only staying in Haiti, but being its future leaders, is a testimony to God's love and miraculous intervention.

"They" are the young men of the Haitian Christian Youth (HCY), a ministry begun by Wes. That is because he saw not the present when he looked into their eyes, but the potential – the future.

Wes explained, "The Genesis to this was my multiple trips to Haiti. Our mission teams were running into young men on the street. They were bright, engaging and helpful." He continued, "It got to the point that I trusted them to help the mission team. They were reasonably fluent in English from talking to the U.S. soldiers during the first occupation (in the early 1990's)."

Wes offered, "I would compensate them, so to speak, by letting them be with the mission team, which was a big treat. We also fed them." As an aside, he offered, "I have never understood why missionaries let Haitians slave all day and not feed them at the end of the day."

He continued, "We came to learn of their desperate family circum-stances and their desire to have an education. Various missionaries would help in different ways. We found they were living in terrible circumstances. Several adults suggested renting a little-two room concrete hobble. It had two 6' by 6' rooms, smaller than a one-car garage. So we did. They lived there over a year. That was about 2001. We prayed for them, arranged for them to go to school and check on them when visiting."

The impact was immediate, noted Wes. "With that level of help, they became shining stars, great hopes for their families because they were going to school and had a hobble."

Wes said the first two young men in HCY were Kalipso and his cousin, Achka. Another, Sandro, began waiting outside the guest house to see if Wes and his team would put him to work that day. "He was so shy, with a very low self-image. But he is very talented. He had paintings for sale." Barbie, Wes's wife, took interest in the paintings and eventually went to see Sandro's work area, accom-panied by "bodyguards" Achka and Kalipso. Wes revealed, "She discovered that Sandro lived in terrible conditions. He was in a mess physically. He lived with his extended family and was not wanted."

Sandro had learned proficient English by studying a dictionary. He wanted money for education, so some of the mission team members agreed to buy his paintings.

Gradually, word spread and more young men would join the others, looking for work and the benefits of getting to know Wes, who says of them, "They are teachable, moldable."

Eventually, Wes and Robert Rice, another committed Haiti servant, rented a larger house. A maximum of eight young men are in it at a time, and Ronald oversees them.

Admittedly, all hasn't gone perfectly. Said Wes, who speaks in the terminology of the businessman he is, "We've had to fire about three or four young men. It's really painful to do, but if they won't follow the rules, are thick-headed and won't apply themselves, I fire them."

Each is required to attend church regularly, study their Bible daily, take English lessons weekly and offer themselves as volun-teers at least once a week. "It's a teamwork approach – all for one and one for all," noted Wes. The young men elect captains, who at the time of my visit were Kalipso and Achka.

HCY still faces challenges. "Every young man is in school, which is an expensive proposition. We make sure they are fed. We come up with a food budget that we strategically distribute. And, there's still a lot of education by the school of hard knocks."

Wes has also had his eyes opened to some things he did not anticipate. He explained, "Their response to volunteer service has been fascinating. You actually have to teach the concept of going out to help somebody that is unknown. It's not part of the culture." But, he continued, "They've really caught on. The older ones are helping younger ones with homework, visiting elders and orphanages, helping paint, that sort of thing."

They have also been introduced to commerce. "They are required to learn a trade to become self-sufficient. We teach them rudimentary business entrepreneurship. We have provided cell phones so that we can keep in touch with them, and taught them computer activities as well as art and painting."

He noted, "They are pretty much self-regulated, so they face the typical issues you would expect. With eight guys living together, especially without socialization advantages, good parenting, and social leadership skills, it can get tense."

Ronald has been a godsend in this regard, noted Wes. "He's a wonderful young man and a very dedicated pastor. We met him at a pastor's conference. He has a sweet wife, no children and a young church. We worshipped there." He added, "It helps to have external controls. Some have been written up for insubordination. That's what Ronald is for, to teach them how to solve the problem, but not solve it for them."

Despite the need for discipline, Wes is also tender-hearted. "Achka has accepted Christ. I love them. They've started calling me father because most of them have never known a father. And that's even after me getting in their face, insisting on accountability. They appreciate it."

Ronald is the one charged with ensuring that the accountability is happening daily. "We do the work that a father would," he explained. "We visit and supervise and teach respect for the place in which they are living. Sometimes we console. We do Bible study to guide them to make good decisions." He continued, "We simply love. We try to fill the gap. We try to help them have a better life. We encourage them. We insist they have a place of worship, to be active in church.

"We train them to do volunteer work, to help others so that the mentality of 'What's in it for me' does not stick with them."

He continued, "The most important thing is to make them aware of God, that He is worthy of reverence and worship – to be submissive to His principles, and to live by the standards that a Christian believes. It is not an easy task to work with people that come out of the street, but we know with the grace of God, prayer and faith, we will overcome the obstacles."

He continued, "That's why before we do anything, we invite the Lord to be in our midst and guide whatever we are about to discuss. My duty is to pray for them and the project. We ask for everyone to join us in that prayer."

Monday evening, I was privileged to meet the young men I had heard so much about. Their stories are so compelling that I really needed to ask each of them only one question – "Would you please tell me your story?"

First though, we had to get comfortable with one another. They also, I would discover after dinner, had such traumatic accounts to recall that they were likely reluctant to visit those dark corners of their hearts and minds where they had shoved the pains, the losses, the abandonment, the day-to-day struggling.

So, to ease into the interviews, we first had dinner together. While I slowly ate, stirring about the assorted offerings on my plate, these seven young men were shoveling in the food voraciously. It soon occurred to me that this was the best – and most substantial – meal they had enjoyed in quite a while. While coming over to meet this friend of Wes may or may not have interested them, they knew that Providence House would provide them with a dinner that was not to be passed up.

Reflective, I quit picking at my food and finished my meal with a renewed thankfulness to God for that which I had too easily taken for granted – food. Indeed, since my return from Haiti, I have developed an entirely new outlook on not only food, but the roof over my head, the mattress under me at night, and all the creature comforts we take for granted.

Anyone who would hear the accounts of these young men would react the same way. Rarely a meal goes by that I do not recall the last evening of my seven days in Haiti.

After we finished dinner, I spoke with Kalipso, Achka, Jean-Marc, Michel, Jimmy, Sandro and Robin. They ranged in ages from 16 to 27, with Jean-Marc being the youngest and Jimmy the oldest.

We went around the table, starting with Kalipso.

He is the fifth of 10 children. When he became old enough to go to school, his parents abandoned him to the streets, where he hooked up with Achka. In the mid 1990's, when U.S. troops were in the nation because of the political instability caused by the return of Jean-Bertrand Aristide, Kalipso would go to the troops for food. In 1996, he met, for the first time, an NDI worker. However, he was skeptical, because earlier missionaries had let him down. He explained, "They promised to pay for my schooling, but didn't. I was discouraged with this."

Still, he remained hopeful. In the late 1990's, Wes came to Haiti. "Wes said he didn't have money to give, but if we'd stick with them and work, then he'd find a way to help. Wes allowed him to be a team guide because he had learned English from the American troops. Kalipso shared, "As I continued to work, Wes decided to start the program HCY. Once we started with that program, a lot of things started happening in our lives. Before that, we had to beg. Now, because we would help with work, we had the privilege of being helped.

"By the grace of God, through Wes and others, we can now be somebody."

Michel, also 23, started his story much like Kalipso and, later, the others. "I was born in a very poor family," he began. The second child of six children, he and his older sister were the only ones sent to school. Then his father died. "I couldn't complete school because we didn't have the money. So, I stayed home to baby sit. With minimum resources, we spent days without eating. My friends

Kalipso and Achka would share. They encouraged me. They would say, 'Trust God. He will work a way.'"

The two friends approached Wes and recommended him for HCY. So, in 2004 he became part of the group and is now in school.

Michel revealed, "I am trusting the Lord. My family looks up to me now. I am the one they have hope in." He explained, "God will use this opportunity to have me become a great leader for my family."

Sandro, 21, spoke hesitantly and emotionally. Several times, he stopped to wipe away tears as he recounted his story. "My mother and father fought because my father was a cheater. I have brothers and sisters I do not know. They split. I stayed with my mother." He continued, "The economic situation was so terrible for my mother that we would go many days without eating. We were always in trouble with the landlord. We couldn't pay. With that, my mother couldn't stand to see me suffer any more. She sent me to live with my cousin who was working. But life was still hard. My cousin couldn't care for me. We still couldn't eat. I felt isolated. I was discouraged about living."

He added, "I love to draw, so I would go help those doing art so that I could get money to eat."

Then, he met Kalipso. "I saw a lot of kids gathering at the hotel to see the missionaries. I saw Kalipso. I saw some Americans buy Haitian art. I asked Kalipso, 'Will you get the Americans to buy art from me so that I can eat?' So, he said, 'Bring some of your things and I'll have them take a look.' He prayed with me that God would help me sell my art. I spoke with Wes and told him about my art. He asked to see it. The next morning, I took my art to Wes inside his hotel. They liked it and asked if they could come to my house to see more. They bought everything that day and gave me money to eat. That day I felt like when the rain falls in the desert."

He continued, "They took samples of my brushes and paint. The next time they came to Haiti, they brought me more brushes and paint. So, to show my appreciation, I tried to always have paintings ready to sell them when they would come back. I would keep in touch with Achka and Kalipso to know when they were coming back."

He admitted, however, "I was still suffering. I was skinny like a broomstick. Others would tease me. The money would only last so long. So, as I got closer to Wes, I explained how hard my life was. He found a sponsor that would sometimes give me money."

Meanwhile, his cousin kicked him out and he found himself homeless. "I slept with friends here and there. The next time I saw Wes, I asked if I could be part of the program. I was on standby. Finally, there was room. I was so happy. I could eat, sleep, bathe and go to school every day."

He concluded, "I consider Wes and his wife, Barbie, as God-sent to save me from the path I was on."

Jean-Marc's story, too, begins with meeting Wes.

"I had a friend that was doing work for NDI. I followed him to the house. I was just standing and watching. Wes told me to help out. At the end of the day, one of the missionaries gave me some money. Sandro was there. I asked Sandro to intercede, to see if I could work with them. Sandro said, 'First, you have to introduce yourself.'" But he was too shy.

Jean Mark continued, "The next day, they were still working. I went. I was digging holes for poles. I worked several days. When others would leave, I would stay and help afterwards. The hard work was appreciated. I asked Kalipso to talk to Wes. He said, 'You talk to the man. That is how you get in the program.' So, I talked to Wes. I told him of my hardships. I told him my mom had hardships. I told him my father left, that they had seven children and that my oldest brother had died. I said I had no hope of support. Wes let me in to the program. My mother is pleased. I live in a small place with lots of others, but I am going to school and eating."

Robin came to Port-au-Prince after his mother died. He lived in a mountain town with his mother and step-father and 11 siblings – eight brothers and three sisters.

He shared, "My mother couldn't pay for school for the whole year. I would go some, then have to stay home and wait until the next year. My mom's husband wouldn't pay for my schooling. I was 16 when my mother died. My step-father didn't want me and nobody would help me. So, I came to Port-au-Prince."

He soon learned that the city was harsh.

"I was living with my brother. He couldn't pay for school or feed me daily because he has his own family, so I would visit my uncle sometimes to eat. It was really a struggle."

He added, "It hurt me that others were going to school and I was unable to go."

Then, like the others, he made the connection to Wes. "One time, when I was sitting in front of my house, Kalipso passed by. Wes was with him, but was in a hurry. He said he'd talk to me later. He did. He took me to the home and spoke with Achka and the others. But they didn't know me and were skeptical. But they said they'd try – by steps. It was a better life. They shared their food, but said I had to prove myself before I could go to school. I did. Shortly thereafter, they accepted me in."

In an understated way, he added simply, "I am happy about that." Asked exactly what he meant, he added a phrase that caused them all to laugh. I asked Joseph why everyone was laughing. Joseph shared, "He said he was happy to be living with his brothers and sisters. They want to know who he thinks are his sisters."

With the laughter, everyone stretched and Joseph suggested we take a break. Only Jimmy and Achka had not yet shared their stories. The break – and the laughter – was well timed, for the last two young men took the longest time to share their stories. After we snooped around the buffet table to see what desserts were left, we all stepped into the courtyard and took a few more minutes to stretch. It was dusk and Achka and Michel, the oldest except for Jimmy, decided they should escort their "little brother" Jean Marc home before it got dark.

So, those of us that remained returned to the dining room table. Jimmy told his story.

"I came to Port-au-Prince when I was three-years-old," he began. "My father did not accept me as his son because I had an eye and an ear problem. I was often sick."

He recounted that he had five siblings, but a sister had died recently.

He continued, "Because my father rejected me, I do not use his last name." He lived with his aunt in Cite Soleil. "I have no memories of my mother. My aunt had no children, so she adopted me when

I was 15. That's when I came to face a real-life crisis." The neighborhood, he explained, was simply too dangerous. It scared him. He was sure he would not live if he stayed there. "A few months later I moved to Delmas 19 because there, there are many missionaries. I would seek them out for food. I would go wherever they would go. That way, I could eat while they were here. I could not speak English but I learned the phrase, 'I have no mother, no father and nothing to eat.'"

He too, envied the other children that were in school. "A friend arranged for me to go to public school. But to stay, I had to work hard to keep good grades. Along with Achka and Kalipso, I was searching for life." He continued, "Because school was downtown, the friend there provided a place to stay. But there was a (physical) distance between me, Achka and Kalipso. They are real friends, because they would visit. Life was not easy. There was no one to look after me. Nobody knew what was going on in my life. My objective was to finish my studies. I finished." In fact, he said, he is the only child in his family to finish school.

But he was disappointed. "I could not go to college. I was not in school anymore. I could not eat. There was no food. On weekends or in the summer there was even less unless a friend would give me a handout."

Kalipso and Achka provided him with the email for Wes, and Jimmy found a way to get to a computer to contact him. In 2003, Wes and the other HCY members let him into the program. He began taking a computer graphics course and is now in college. "After my first year I have good grades. I'm so grateful for this program. If not for it, I would not have a future. I have a different mindset. I can see a future. Now, my family looks up to me. I now have necessities. I do some small business ventures and help my family. Anything God starts, He will finish. We will one day be the leaders of Haiti. The future of this country is in the youth, especially with this program."

They are demonstrating leadership, as Kalipso and Achka are showing the entrepreneurial inclinations of their mentor, Wes. They buy old cars, repair them, and then sell them at a profit.

Achka was the last to speak. Perhaps because he was one of the first two in the program, or perhaps because he had heard what the others had not told, or maybe for both those reasons, he told the longest of the stories.

It began with the familiar phrase, "I was raised in a poor family."

He is the fourth of 10 children, two that have died. He revealed, "In 1991, my father died. My mother was struggling. Our family had no hope of having any breaks in our lives. My mother collected plastics to sell to feed us, but there were 12 of us living in one room with dirt floors. When it rained, we would all get a pot to throw the water out. That is something I will never forget if I get to help lead Haiti in the future."

He continued with the story. "I remember one rainy day. My two youngest siblings were on a bed. As the rain was falling, a flood came. The wall caved in and fell on the children. They were injured. There was no way to get them to the hospital. Right then and there, my mother crumbled down and cried out, 'Jesus, save us from this misery.' This is engraved in my heart as a reminder."

His mind drifted to 1994. "I would search for pennies or whatever to get food. I would collect aluminum and brass to sell by the weight. It would give us a little money for food. That's what I did everyday." He was 11 then. He continued, "We used to pray, 'God please make a way for us, a better life.' In 1994, when I saw helicopters over Haiti, I saw it as an answered prayer. It was the American troops coming to disarm the Haitian military."

He shared, "I went to the industrial park to see what was going on. They would not let Haitians near because of security. I would go back the next day. Troops would throw us bags of food, but the older guys would get violent, so I would grab a bag and run home. Each day I would go back to ask for food. Sometimes, they would not give it, so we would go through the troops' garbage to find food or dollar bills."

Because of the behavior of some of the older male Haitians, the American troops became embittered, said Achka, and would mistreat the Haitians. "They did this because some people were stealing the belongings of the troops."

Finally, missionaries came back. "So, we would go to them instead of the troops. We asked at the hotel where missionaries stayed. We found some. But they did not know who we were."

However, because he and Kalipso had learned some English from the troops, the missionaries slowly, cautiously, but eventually came to trust them. He explained, "Kalipso and I stuck with that group of missionaries that would come into the lobby and would go with them to help them."

However, the hotel owner didn't want them coming into the hotel, so they'd wait outside. "Soon, the missionaries were taking us to church."

Still, some were suspicious, since they rotated in and out. "They got in a vehicle to go to a village to work. We asked to help, but the leaders wouldn't allow it. So we started running after the missionary vehicle. We lost the vehicle, but we kept asking people if they had seen the Americans. We finally found them. We went inside and they let us work. They gave us a ride back. We told them it was an answered prayer. They, too, took us to church. We were not hoping for that. But we exchanged addresses. We tried to learn more English. I learned the phrase, 'Give me what you don't use.'"

Achka revealed, "We would identify a missionary to 'adopt' to ask for things. We stayed friends and worked with them. Then Wes came and heard our testimonies. We started to work with Wes." He continued, "When I turned 18, my mother kicked me out because she could not feed me. I went to live with a friend. I talked to Kalipso. I wanted to talk to Wes, but it was too big of a burden. I asked Kalipso, 'Do you think he would rent us a place to live?'"

They appealed to other missionaries they knew to advocate for them with Wes. They did. HCY was born. Said Achka, "It is a great joy and a great pleasure to live with these guys. We won't be together forever, as we begin to graduate. But for now, I am joyful. I want to thank God that he put in Wes's heart to help with this program and the many programs in Haiti he does."

Sandro added, "In the midst of all the bad press about Haiti, you came here. Each of us has a sad story. We are thankful for Wes Morgan, Barbie and the whole staff at NDI that they see the good news. If not for them, we don't know where we would be, especially the younger guys. Most of us were involved in bad things. If not for NDI, we would be hopeless. We are happy and proud to know that we have friends in the United States that have an interest in our future. They showed us how to live. Not only do we benefit, but our families do also. They have it better. They see us and have hope. They now have a better way of thinking. Now we have visions, goals, and objectives of where we want to go."

Jimmy, the oldest, added, "The money and time they invest in us, in a few years, God willing, will bring forth fruit. We cannot reward them, but their reward will come from above. We are the future leaders of Haiti. They had faith in all of us that we will be leaders."

Holy Communion

*"And I believe what I believe/Is what makes me what
I am/I did not make it, no it is making me/It is the
very truth of God and not/The invention of any man."
(Lyrics from "Creed" by the late Rich Mullins).*

Monday was my last full day in Haiti. It was also, unquestionably, the most exhausting – physically and emotionally.
From beginning the day visiting orphans that had been rescued
from unspeakable horrors to spending hours around the dinner
table taking notes as the young men of the HCY recounted their
harrowing and heartbreaking – yet ultimately uplifting – stories, the
day left me spent.

I was both elated and crushed that this would be my last day of
spending time with these humble servants of Christ. Elated because
I missed my family; crushed because I had been so blessed and made
so many new friends that I did not want to leave them, particularly
since I didn't know when – or if – I would be returning.

Perhaps that is why I woke that morning earlier than usual. Or
perhaps the relatively relaxing weekend had allowed me to charge
my batteries enough to greet the day with spiritual vigor and enthusiasm even though I was physically exhausted. Whatever the reason,
I was up early enough to spend extra time in my Bible; I was also
led to reflect more in response to my reading in the Chambers book
than I had most other mornings while there.

This day's study began, "If the Son of God is born into my mortal flesh, is His holy innocence and simplicity and oneness with the Father getting a chance to manifest itself in me?" I drew an arrow over to the space for journaling and simply wrote, "That is my desire." Little did I know, of course, that this would be a day in which I would see holy innocence (the orphans at CRES) and oneness with the Father (Ronald and the HCY) modeled so that my prayer, expressed in the lives of others, would be answered.

Reading further, I underlined, "Am I continually saying with amazement to my common-sense life – why do you want to turn me off here? Don't you know that I must be about my Father's business?" It seemed God's Spirit was speaking to my body.

I continued reading. Next, I underlined, "Oh, the clamor of these days! Everyone is clamoring – for what? For the Son of God to be put to death. There is no room here for the Son of God just now, no room for quiet holy communion with the Father. Is the Son of God praying in me or am I dictating to Him? Is he ministering in me as He did in the days of His flesh?" As I read this, it was barely dawn. I realized that I was blessed to enjoy "holy communion" with our Lord. I also realized that the past several days of spending time with Christians who, I concluded, must be very much like the first century Christians, had been a time of God ministering to me just as He did when He walked the earth. I had witnessed faith and obedience unlike anything I had ever seen – or have yet to fully realize – in the United States. For in the U.S., I realized – and see ever clearer now – many are clamoring for Jesus to be put to death. Indeed, this is the case in a very first century way. For, not only does the culture reject Christ, but so do significant segments of the Church. Those Christians who live their faith through a relationship with Christ, not as a ritualistic religion, are treated as oddities. Within their own churches, they are often silenced. If they speak of holiness and surrender, of obedience to the Great Commission, of faith through grace, of recalling our own journey before we came to know Christ, they are shunned. Why? They are "calling out" the Church to make room for Christ, but we have filled our lives with so many false idols – of self-sufficiency, of industry, of sensuality, of commercialism, of vain rituals, of celebrity – that we have no room for the Son of God.

But not so these humble Haitians.

I read next, "The more one knows of the inner life of God's ripest saints, the more one sees what God's purpose is – 'filling up that which is behind the affliction of Christ.'" In response, I wrote, "As for me, this morning I am completely exhausted and in significant pain with a sore back and aching muscles. But now I have a much better understanding of the 'afflictions of Christ.'"

As I reflected upon that last phrase, a seemingly random thought entered my mind. I recalled the endless promotion within Christian churches when Mel Gibson's "Passion of the Christ" was released and thought of how so many had said, "This is the greatest witnessing tool you can use to win your friends to Christ." I wrote, "Is this really identifying with Christ? If a movie is your best witnessing tool for a friend, you are neither much of a friend nor a disciple."

Instead, I thought, living a life surrendered to Christ is the best witness. But then, do we have room for that?

As one considers Jehu and all that he sacrifices, it is a fair question.

As I went upstairs at the end of the day, short on time and too tired to write of all that I had experienced on my sixth day in Haiti, I opened my Bible to Acts 4, where we read of how the believers share their possessions. I intended to jot a note in my Bible to remind myself to weave this story into the account of the HCY. However, that page of my Bible has a profile on Barnabas. I read it and underlined this phrase: "...when everyone else suspected and rejected him." The account, of course, is of Barnabas encouraging Paul when everyone else wanted nothing to do with him. I wrote above the profile, "Wes and Haitian Christian Youth." For that was each of their stories. When everyone else rejected them, Wes accepted them. By extension, Ronald, as the HCY director, has done the same. Jehu, as well, has done the same with the orphans of CRES.

This, I thought, as I closed my Bible and then my eyes, is what Chambers meant when he said that God's "ripest saints" reflect the "affliction of Christ."

Day 7: Tuesday, August 9

A New Direction

Another Good Friend

"A man of many companions may come to ruin, but there is a friend who sticks closer than a brother"
(Proverbs 18: 24).

My first meeting with Joseph did not go as planned. In fact, the first planned meeting didn't happen at all.

Joseph, who served as my guide, translator, and ultimately friend for my week in Haiti, was supposed to greet me at the airport. While I had been occasionally contemplating what kind of person he was and how God was going to work with us and through us, I had more immediate concerns. In short, as I exited the airport terminal, baggage in tow and not one recognizable face in the crowd of people, I was anticipating meeting Joseph as much for the security he offered as for any companionship. When one sees U.N. troops holding very large guns in every corner of the airport, one does, very much, want to see a friendly face. So, I was waiting for Joseph to recognize the NDI shirt I was wearing and immediately call out my name.

But he did not.

Instead, Joseph, because of his car troubles, had to send a surrogate. Even though I had not yet met Joseph, he had gotten me there, for he was on the other end of the phone, relaying directions to his friend. So, even though an obstacle was put in his place (which surprised neither of us, for the spiritual warfare in Port-au-Prince is almost palpable), Joseph still looked out for my welfare as well as any friend would.

That is not surprising, though, for we are more than friends – we are brothers – through our relationships with Jesus Christ.

This is not a trite expression, though it is often trivialized. Indeed, a week later, as Joseph accompanied me up to the very last step that he could in the airport before I went through customs, I experienced the pangs of sorrow that accompany separating from a dear friend or family member. God truly had forged a bond between us as only He can – especially in such a short period of time.

I knew it from the first morning when I warned Joseph that I would talk his ear off as I do with my wife over breakfast, and he just smiled.

He was concerned for my comfort and for my well-being. He invited his friend Stanley to accompany us on most of our trips, an added blessing, as he was always smiling and holding a hand out – literally – to the U.S. citizen with an unstable back and knees, and quickly graying hair.

Our seven days were frenzied, beginning with an interview after dinner with Pastor Dieuseul. Every morning began with breakfast at 7, followed by a full day of interviews, visits and even a bit of sight-seeing thrown in.

The day generally did not end until the last story was filed, some-times as late as 11 or so. With the hectic schedule, the traffic noise, the rush to do interviews and get stories filed, Joseph and I really didn't have much time to talk. During meals and between stops, or as we gazed at the harbor from high above the city, we'd get a few moments to talk. Yet, after a week, I knew there was more to be told by this man who humbly, gently and yet assertively, looked out for my every need. So, with the luggage packed, we sat and Joseph told of his life in Christ, the love he has for Haiti and how these two passions merge.

He shared, "I was born in a Christian family. Ever since I could remember, my father was a minister. At a very young age, we were involved in the church. I didn't understand it, but it was fun." Indeed, though his father is now deceased, Joseph often visits what he still affectionately calls, "my father's church."

It did not take him long to understand he had his own decision to make. He recalled that it was in unusual circumstances that he came to faith it Christ. "I remember I was maybe seven-years-old. We were playing church. One day we were playing church and I received the Holy Ghost. When we stopped that day, something came over us. We all felt it. It was my first experience with that," explained Joseph.

With both of his parents being musically inclined, he was easily encouraged to be likewise and was playing the flute at age nine. He noted, "When I was 13, I started to teach music theory in my father's church." They would travel to other churches to sing, and at 15, he became the church's band leader. However, the political unrest in Haiti created too much stress for his mother. He recalled, "My mother couldn't take the gunshots anymore." So, in 1988 they moved to Maryland.

Joseph said, "I continued to perform in my music ministry. I felt great, felt it was my calling to teach music to the churches. In Maryland, I started from scratch two bands, one in a Haitian church and one in an African-American church. As I grew up in my faith in the Lord, I felt at my church they wanted me to be more involved in the ministry."

Yet, he acknowledged, "As an immediate witness of my father's ministry, I saw his sufferings. I saw how he suffered for the Gospel. My vow was, I think music is good enough for me. I don't want to go any further than that. I can be a good saint in the church, a good brother. I would help them, but I did not want responsibility other than music. As the pastor wanted me to be more involved, I decided to move, just to not be more involved."

So, in June of 1996, he moved to Florida with his wife, Marie Carmel, whose father pastored a church in Delray Beach. Smiling, Joseph continued, "So, I ran away from a bigger responsibility in Maryland and came to Florida and the same responsibilities were waiting for me." He added, "Her father told me you need to be more involved than in music. Somebody else can teach music. You can teach music as well, but I feel God has more that he wants you to do. I want you to be more involved.' Out of courtesy, I said yes. But in my mind, I knew that was not my plan."

He continued, "In February, 1997, God shook that church. The same way Satan went to God and asked for permission to test Job, the same thing happened at our church. Satan got into a few of the leaders of the church and allowed them to stir some division in the church. In an assembly with over 300 members, about half of them left the church at once. Each of the leaders took a handful to start their own church. That really hurt my father-in-law. It affected him physically, so he was hospitalized. He had a nervous breakdown. So I had to step up and accept the responsibilities." He added, "Temporarily, because I knew in my mind this was not my calling. This is what I had been telling myself."

Joseph acknowledged, "Although I was acting as a pastor, that was not in my heart. I would slack up sometime. I wouldn't make the effort to go to church, because that is not what I wanted."

He continued, "So God saw me being so stubborn that in April 2000, he gave me a wake up call. I was driving to school one afternoon and I felt a tingling on the right side of my face. I was driving with my left hand. My right arm was on the arm rest. As I felt the tingling, I raised my hand to touch my face. I knew that was want I wanted to do, but nothing happened. I could not raise my arm. I was shocked.

"God was right there with me. He allowed me to make a U-turn. I drove about five minutes with my left foot and left hand to the Coral Springs hospital. I parked the car, opened the door and tried to drag myself out of the car because I was numb on my right side. The hospital personnel put me in a wheelchair, took me inside, and took my blood pressure. The nurse picked up phone said, 'Code yellow! I need a bed now!' She got my name, wife's name and phone number. That is all I remember."

Hours later, he woke up hooked to "all kinds of wiring and oxygen" with his wife and mother-in-law at his bedside. He added, "They told me I had a minor stroke."

He spent eight months without working, and ended up taking 12 prescriptions, with one written to balance the effects of the others and so forth. "I was able to do movement with my arm, but I had no strength. I couldn't use my right hand to eat and was slow in my speech."

Then, after the eight months, something the doctors can not explain happened. He was healed.

Joseph explained, "I went to church. It was a Wednesday night prayer service. As the Spirit of the Lord was moving in that service, one of the sisters, something told her to come and raise my right arm. She was praying, 'God put life in this arm. He is your servant. He needs his arm to work for you.' I could feel the power running from the tip of my finger down to my feet. I felt something different happen to me that day. As soon as they started to sing, I hopped on the keyboard and was playing it, with tears in my eyes, thanking him for the healing."

He observed, "Ever since then, I have changed my line of thought. I now say, 'God, not my will, but let your will be done.' From then on, even the doctors could not see what happened. I never used those pills anymore."

Indeed, during the seven days in Port-au-Prince, Joseph drove a large truck, easily negotiating the steep and narrow streets, something possible only by a driver in complete control of his faculties.

"So," concluded Joseph, "I decided that I felt that God really wanted me to be more involved in the ministry. I started to feel that I needed to do something in the mission field." With that thought in mind, he recalled a Haitian pastor he had met in the states in 1999, Michel Morriset from Ebenezer Mission in Gonaives. "He too encouraged me to be more involved in the ministry. So I started to travel more to Haiti and help him out with information technology, hooking up the Internet, working on broken computers. We got to be very close. Everything he was doing, he would ask for my input."

That relationship led to what Joseph called "another divine appointment from God." Joining Morriset at a church in Gonaives in February of 2004, Joseph met Wes.

Wes, who was ill with cancer, came with some food for the relief program after the flood. Joseph recalled, "On Sunday morning, he stood up and gave his life's testimony, his challenges, his faith and said he believes God will let him live, that he does not feel he has done enough for God just yet."

He continued, "After the service was over, I went up to him to encourage him in his faith. I told him that God is able and I am not just saying that, because he had healed me from my illness. After I gave him my testimony, the first words that came out of his mouth were, 'Do you need a job?' I was stunned."

Joseph added, "My response was, 'I don't know if I need a job.' But my thought was that I had just decided to involve myself full time in the ministry without really knowing how my income or expenses would be covered, but I trusted the Lord. And here is this man, asking me if I need a job." Still, he struggled. "In my mind, I thought maybe a job will tie me up again. I didn't know if it was God telling me it is now time, or if the devil was trying to tie me up to keep me out of the mission field. So I didn't give him an answer."

However, Joseph shared, "God put in his heart to learn more. He asked the pastor for more information. He got more interested. So, he left and went back to the states and I was still in Haiti when I received a call from him and he told me he was coming back and asked if I was willing to spend a week so we could get to know each other. I said I will make myself available. So we did, in March."

Another NDI representative, Crawford Hitt, also was coming to Haiti. Wes asked him if he would work with Crawford for five days. "I said, 'I'm here already. I'll be waiting on you.'"

After that, he was invited to visit NDI's headquarters to meet with the leadership team. "They really made me feel at home. I really felt the Lord had put us together. I have never regretted or had any doubts that it was a divine appointment."

Joseph wants to do much more for Haiti. "My mother started a clinic in my father's memory. She would like to have a clinic in each of the satellite churches. My goal is to help her fulfill that dream, and perhaps build one of the best hospitals for Haiti." Indeed, he and others have established a nonprofit in Florida towards achieving that objective. He said, "Hopefully, by the grace of God we will find a way to make this happen."

He added, "This is my long term goal, to build the hospital, fully equipped. In the meantime, my goal is to strengthen the local pastors in my father's satellite churches."

And there is the work with NDI. "Most of their partners don't speak English. Also, especially with some of the transactions, they feel more comfortable knowing there is a Haitian-American that will relay their message to NDI. They feel that their partnership with NDI will be more efficient.

"We hope that by the grace of God we will accomplish a lot more. He is a giving God. We believe with all the trouble that Haiti is going through, with those many different programs that NDI is involved with, they will contribute to the changes of the better Haiti. As we all realize, Haiti's problem is spiritual. We need Jesus to change the situation and heal Haiti."

He concluded, "Everyone affiliated with NDI that I have worked with so far has been a blessing to me."

That is probably because Kingdom appointments make for the most joyous of relationships. That is certainly the case with Joseph, another good friend brought into my life by the Savior.

Tearing Myself Away

"After we had torn ourselves away from them, we put out to sea sailed straight to Cos"

(Acts 21:1).

Much of what you just read about Joseph was news to me, even though I had spent the week with him. In part, that is because Joseph is a humble man; however, it is also because we both were focused on the task before us – recounting the stories of just a few Christians in Port-au-Prince. Though you have read of only about two dozen believers – of varying ages and spiritual maturity – I am confident that they are indicative of the state of the Church not only in the capitol, but all of Haiti. That is because I have talked to numerous other ministry leaders that partner with Haitians. But mostly it is because of how meeting them changed my life.

Their humility, their kindness, their openness – their meekness – forced me to consider God from outside the U.S. experience.

As I parted with Joseph at the airport – he went as far as he was allowed, ensuring I got through customs without incident – I thought of what the Apostle Luke wrote when he left Ephesus for Jerusalem. "After we had torn ourselves away from them…" (Acts 21:1a). We hugged at the door leading to the security checkpoint. Just as the brothers we are, we reluctantly let go of one another. I quickly turned. My heart was torn.

I grabbed a seat and opened my Bible. I began again at Acts. Because it is The Leadership Bible, each book begins with an over-arching leadership principle. This one read, "By his Spirit, God works through ordinary people to accomplish his work in the world. Those who open themselves to the Spirit's call find new directions (Acts 9) and new purpose for their lives as leaders." I underlined the words "new direction" and wrote, "8/9/05 Read while sitting in airport in Port-au-Prince after week of reporting on activities of Christians here on behalf on New Directions International."

Little did I know, of course, that my own life would take such a new direction as a result of the trip. Knowing the ministry as I do now, though, I am not surprised. For their model of ministry – evangelism, partnership and development – is indeed biblical.

Earlier, I noted that the last line from the "Utmost for His Highest" study for this last day I spent in Haiti asked, "Are we living in such human dependence upon Jesus Christ that His life is being manifested moment by moment?" That question challenged me to consider whether I was living as a bond-slave of Christ.

It is appropriate to ask it again, just as God providentially posed it to me as my Haiti visit was drawing to a close.

As I complete this book, it has now been more than a year since I visited Haiti. Yet, the memories of that seventh day, that morning – that week – remain vivid. One can appreciate how, years after Christ ascended into heaven, His disciples could cast vivid accounts of His days on earth. When God moves in your life, you don't forget it. Each day had begun with Bible study and the Chambers book, writing in response to what God was revealing.

Of course, it was through His Haitian believers that He moved the clearest and spoke the loudest.

I can see the people, smell the odors, hear the noise, feel the gravel under my feet on the uneven and steep roads, hear the chatter among the Providence House staff in Creole, recall the bouncing of the truck, remember the stifling heat and humidity, and most importantly, the love of those I met.

That last morning, I consciously cleared my mind and geared my senses to absorb all that was around me; I programmed my mind, so to speak, to recall the moments. I knew also it was to be a relatively leisurely morning. I had only to interview Joseph in the five hours from the time I had finished packing until we would be leaving for the airport. So, I had plenty of time to read my Bible and my study. Hence, the notes I made that morning were extensive. I don't know that they are any more poignant than those of the other mornings, for God's Spirit truly moved like the wind – I knew it was always present, but I did not know when its force would suddenly increase, or from what direction it would come. I did not know how or where it would move me; I just knew it would.

So, in addition to the last line from Chambers' study for the morning, I highlighted several passages. The first thing I did was circle the Scripture reference: "Father, I thank Thee that Thou hast heard Me" (John 11:41).

I thought back to the previous August, when in Virginia, God had placed in my heart the overwhelming desire to leave the United States to see what Christians faced in other lands. During that year, I had often wondered if God was going to hear me. I should not have, I know. But I was fearful that my natural affinity for adventure had led to that desire, rather than God's Spirit. Yet, I recalled how I was moved during that visit to World Help. I knew also how J.L. had challenged me. I knew the Scripture, "Delight yourself in the Lord and he will give you the desires of your heart" (Psalm 37:4). I know to delight yourself means to seek and do His will (though that is not all that it means), and that if and when you do so, He will place the desires on your heart that align with your God-given gifts, abilities, talents and interests. Consequently, what we desire is what He wills for us – for His purposes.

For the believer, this is an incredible sense of joy and security. And that is what I felt this morning, as I read that Scripture. I was so thankful that He had heard me. Yet, it was an adventurous time. It was what every journalist dreams of. I report upon Great Commission efforts. I was on the front lines of that work. I couldn't – professionally – have asked for more.

Spiritually, I had experienced more than I could ever have imagined. God, surely, had heard me.

I read on. "Is the Son of God getting His chance in me?" Chambers asked. He continued, "Is the direct simplicity of the life of God's Son being worked out exactly as it was worked out in His historic life? When I come in contact with the occurrences of life as an ordinary human being, is the prayer of God's Eternal Son to His Father being prayed in me? 'In that day ye shall ask in My name....' What day? The day when the Holy Ghost has come to me and made me effectually one with my Lord." He added, "Is the Lord Jesus Christ being abundantly satisfied in your life or have you got a spiritual strut on?"

It was a perplexing question. Why? I had grown in my relationship with Christ in a manner surpassing anything I could have imagined. I considered that a privilege, so "strutting" in that knowledge was a danger. Still, as I considered those I was soon to leave behind, I was humbled to think that their faith is as great as their circumstances are uncertain.

I read on. "Our ordinary wits never worship God unless they are transfigured by the indwelling Son of God."

I wrote in response, "In the case of the last sentence, I can say this is true regarding the Haitian Christians I have met. Because of their example, I hope and pray it shall always be true for me – always." I continued, "I am ambivalent about leaving Haiti. I miss my family greatly. Yet, it is my prayer, that if it be God's will, I would be an instrument of His peace."

An astonishing thing happened next. Though I had been reading in the book of Acts, as I prayed in response to my Utmost study, God's Spirit impressed me to read from the sixth chapter of Ephesians, for I couldn't help but think that the greatest enemies my new friends faced were spiritual. I got about halfway through the chapter when I read, "Stand firm then, with the belt of truth buckled around your waist, with the breastplate of righteousness in place, and with you feed fitted with the readiness that comes from the gospel of peace" (Ephesians 6: 14-15). I put an asterisk beside the 15th verse.

The bottom third of this page in the Bible was blank since it was the end of this letter of Paul. So I put another asterisk there and wrote, in dateline form, "Aug. 9, 2005 PORT-AU-PRINCE, Haiti – This morning, before opening this section, I prayed that if God willed, He would allow me to be an instrument of His peace in Haiti. Little did I know that God would answer this prayer so quickly and clearly." Indeed, at the risk of seeming to put a "spiritual strut" on, I humbly pray that this account will inspire Christians to work for peace in Haiti.

How gracious is our Lord. That is what my experience with Haitian Christians taught me. Our Lord was – is – relational. I learned to be a bond-slave in Haiti through these ordained – and "ordinary" – relationships. While most readers have not personally met these folks, I trust their faith is so compelling that you are convicted to pray that God will search your heart and reveal to you how you can be more surrendered to Him, so that you may be an instrument of His peace wherever you are.

Reporting all
that God Has Done

"On arriving there, they gathered the church together and reported all that God had done through them and how he had opened the door of faith to the Gentiles"

(Acts 14: 26-27).

B efore I left for Haiti, I had no idea what I was getting into. But I was excited.

When I returned from Haiti, I was overcome with the magnitude of what I had seen and experienced, and how to respond to it.

What does one do in the face of such suffering? I have worked in public schools, in local ministry, and as a coach and mentor. In many instances, the never-ending needs have been heartbreaking and mind-boggling.

So in response to Haiti, all I could do was ask of God, "What was *that* all about? What am I supposed to do? What do you want me to learn?"

I recalled that my search for Shining Lights had led me there. As Jesus taught, the purpose of letting our light shine is so that God may be glorified. Hence, I concluded that the story of these Haitian Christians must be told, as they too are Shining Lights. I believe there is precedent for conveying such tales.

At the end of the 14th chapter of Acts, I underlined these verses – in flight, as I "sailed" home: "From Attalia they sailed back to Antioch, where they had been committed to the grace of God for the work they had now completed. On arriving there, they gathered the church together and reported all that God had done through them and how he had opened the door of faith to the Gentiles" (Acts 14: 26-27). I concluded I was to do the same.

This is my effort to "gather the church together" so that it may hear what God is doing through our brothers and sisters in Haiti. I can report to you that God has worked through them to widen the door of my faith.

I pray their stories do the same for you.

Printed in the United States
69627LV00003B/49-84